QBasic Functions and S[...]

NAME	DESCRIPTION	CHAPTER	NAME	DESCRIPTION	CHAPTER
'	Starts a remark	4	LEN()	Tells the amount of memory needed to store something	12
ASC()	Returns the ASCII value of a character	12	LINE	Draws a line	26
BEEP	Beeps the computer	8	LOCATE	Moves the cursor	8
CALL	Calls a subroutine	24	LPRINT	Prints stuff to the printer	5
CINT()	Rounds a number off to the nearest integer	11	MID$()	Returns the middle part of a string	12
CHR$()	Prints an ASCII character	12	NEXT	Starts the next run of a FOR loop	16
CIRCLE	Draws a circle	26			
CLNG()	Converts a number to a long	11	OPEN	Opens a file	20
CLOSE	Closes a file	20	PRESET	Turns off a pixel	26
CLS	Clears the screen	5	PRINT	Prints stuff to the screen	5
COLOR	Changes the color of your screen and text	8	PSET	Turns on a pixel	26
			PUT #	Puts a record in a file	21
DATA	Stores data	17	RANDOMIZE	Seeds RND()	11
DATE$	Returns the date	12	READ	Gets data from a DATA line	17
DEF FN	Lets you define your own functions	23	REM	Starts a remark	4
DIM	Defines an array	18	RETURN	Returns from a GOSUB chunk	22
DO LOOP	Repeats a chunk of code	15	RIGHT$()	Returns the right part of a string	12
ELSE	Works with IF; executes code if something *isn't* true	13	RND()	Returns a random number	11
END	Ends a program or a section of code	4	SCREEN	Changes the format of your screen	26
EOF()	Tells whether its the end of a file	20	SELECT CASE	Executes different chunks of code depending on a value	14
FIX()	Lops off the decimal part of a number	11	SOUND	Your computer makes a sound	25
			STEP	Used to increment FOR loops	16
FOR	Repeats a chunk of code a set number of times	16	SUB	Marks the beginning of a subroutine	24
GET #	Gets a record from a file	21	TAB()	Moves the cursor in a set number of positions	8
GOSUB	Sends QBasic to a different chunk of code	22	THEN	Goes with the IF statement	13
IF	Executes a block of code if something is true	13	TIME$	Returns the time	12
			TIMER	Returns the number of seconds since midnight	11
INPUT	Gets stuff from the user	7			
INPUT #	Gets stuff from a file	20	TYPE	Defines a special data type	21
INT()	Returns the smallest integer closest to a number	11	UCASE$()	Makes a string all uppercase letters	12
LCASE$()	Makes a string all lowercase letters	12	WHILE	The test statement for a DO LOOP	15
LEFT$()	Returns the left part of a string	12	WRITE #	Writes to a file	20

For more information just flip the card

QBasic's Menu Bar Selections

MENU OPTION	DESCRIPTION
File	File-related commands that operate on your program such as loading a program from disk, saving the program you enter to disk, and erasing the current program from memory.
Edit	Includes options that aid in adding, changing, and deleting text from the current program.
View	Lets you move between QBasic's editing window and the program's output screen and subroutines.
Search	Performs search and replace functions that let you find any text even in the longest of programs.
Run	The most-used menu option on the menu bar. This pull-down menu includes the Start command that runs whatever program you type in memory.
Debug	Helps you get the errors out of your program.
Options	Lets you customize the editor and screen.
Help	QBasic provides a rich assortment of online electronic help. Instead of having a QBasic Reference manual open in front of you, you can select from the various help-related topics to find anything you need about the editor or about QBasic.

The QBasic Shortcut Keys

SHORTCUT KEY	MENU OPTION
F1	Help	Topic
F2	View	SUBs...
F3	Search	Repeat Last Find
F4	View	Output Screen
F5	Run	Continue
F8	Debug	Step
F9	Debug	Toggle Breakpoint
F10	Debug	Procedure Step
Del	Edit	Clear
Shift+F1	Help	Using Help
Shift+F5	Run	Start
Shift+Del	Edit	Cut
Ctrl+Ins	Edit	Copy
Shift+Ins	Edit	Paste

VGA SCREEN Mode Values

MODE	DESCRIPTION
0	Text resolution at 80 rows by 25 columns; 16 colors for CGA or EGA, 64 colors for EGA or VGA.
1	320 columns and 200 rows of pixels and up to 4 colors at once.
2	640 columns and 200 rows of pixels and up to 2 colors at once.
7	320 columns and 200 rows of pixels and up to 16 colors at once.
8	640 columns and 200 rows of pixels and up to 16 colors at once.
9	640 columns and 350 rows of pixels and up to 16 colors at once.
10	640 columns and 350 monochrome (one-color) pixels.
11	640 columns and 480 rows of pixels and up to 2 colors at once.
12	640 columns and 480 rows of pixels and up to 16 colors at once.
13	320 columns and 200 rows of pixels and up to 256 colors at once.

The QBasic COLOR Values Chart

COLOR NUMBER	COLOR
0	Black
1	Blue
2	Green
3	Cyan
4	Red
5	Magenta
6	Brown
7	White
8	Gray
9	Light Blue
10	Light Green
11	Light Cyan
12	Light Red
13	Light Magenta
14	Yellow
15	Bright White

The QBasic Order of Operators

LEV.	OPERATOR
1	Parenthesis
2	Exponentiation (^)
3	Negation (-)
4	Multiplication (*), division (/)
5	Integer division (\)
6	Modulus (MOD)
7	Addition (+), subtraction (-)
8	Relational operators (=, <, >, <=, >=, <>)
9	NOT
10	AND
11	OR
12	XOR

Absolute Beginner's Guide to
QBasic™

Absolute Beginner's Guide to QBasic™

Greg Perry

SAMS
PUBLISHING

A Division of Prentice Hall Computer Publishing
11711 North College, Carmel, Indiana 46032 USA

For Jerry Pournelle, whose stories I read
and whose articles I *always* agree with.

Copyright © 1993 by Sams Publishing

Trademarks

Publisher
Richard K. Swadley

Acquisitions Manager
Jordan Gold

Acquisitions Editor
Stacy Hiquet

Development Editor
Dean Miller

Senior Editor
Tad Ringo

Production Editor
Cheri Clark

Editorial Coordinators
Rebecca S. Freeman
Bill Whitmer

Editorial Assistants
Rosemarie Graham
Sharon Cox

Technical Reviewer
Keith Davenport

Marketing Manager
Greg Wiegand

Cover Designer
Jean Bisesi

Illustrator
Kevin Spear

**Director of Production
and Manufacturing**
Jeff Valler

Production Manager
Corinne Walls

Imprint Manager
Matthew Morrill

Book Designer
Michele Laseau

Production Analyst
Mary Beth Wakefield

Proofreading/Indexing Coordinator
Joelynn Gifford

Graphics Image Specialists
Dennis Sheehan
Sue VandeWalle

Production
Diana Bigham
Christine Cook
Lisa Daugherty
Terri Edwards
Mitzi Foster Gianakos
Dennis Clay Hager
Howard Jones
John Kane
Sean Medlock
Juli Pavey
Linda Quigley
Michelle Self
Barbara Webster
Donna Winter
Phil Worthington

Indexer
John Sleeva

Overview

Contents

Part III QBasic and Math

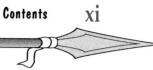

Part IV QBasic Takes Control

Part V Lots of Lists, Tables, and Storage

Appendixes

Acknowledgments

I want to thank Dean Miller, who edits with style, Keith Davenport, who edits with accuracy, and Cheri Clark, who edits with grace. They made this book into what I could not.

Stacy Hiquet, Jordan Gold, and Richard Swadley continue to ask me back to Sams Publishing, and I am so very grateful that they do. I hope my sluggish writing speeds and my inability to tackle a wide range of writing subjects don't turn them off too much.

In the end, my beautiful bride, Jayne, and my parents, Glen and Bettye, keep me going.

About the Author

Greg Perry is a speaker and writer in both the programming and the applications sides of computing. He is known for bringing programming topics down to the beginner's level. Perry has been a programmer and trainer for the past 15 years. He received his first degree in computer science, and then he received a master's degree in corporate finance. Besides writing, he teaches, consults, and lectures across the country, including at the acclaimed Software Development programming conferences. Perry is the author of 18 other computer books, including *Absolute Beginner's Guide to Programming, Absolute Beginner's Guide to C, Turbo C++ Programming 101, Moving from C to C++,* and *QBasic Programming 101* (all published by Sams Publishing). In addition, he has published articles in several publications, such as *PC World, Data Training,* and *Inside First Publisher.* In his spare time, he gives lectures on traveling in Italy, his second-favorite place to be.

Introduction

Do you think you'll *never* be able to program computers? Would you like to learn QBasic but just don't have the time or energy? Is your old, worn-out computer in need of new programs to spice up its circuits? This book is just what the doctor ordered!

Absolute Beginner's Guide to QBasic breaks the commonality of computer books by talking directly at your level while not talking down to you. *Absolute Beginner's Guide to QBasic* is like your best friend sitting next to you teaching QBasic. This book attempts to *express* without having to *impress*. *Absolute Beginner's Guide to QBasic* talks to you in plain language, not in computerese. This book, with its short chapters, line drawings, and often humorous straight talk, makes your trip through the maze of QBasic programming faster and friendlier and easier than any other book available today.

Who Is This Book For?

This is a beginner's book. If you have never programmed before, this book is for you. No knowledge of any programming concept is assumed. If you can't even spell *PC*, you can learn to program QBasic with this book.

The term *beginner* has different meanings at different times. You might be new to computers. You might never have programmed before. You might have programmed in other languages but are a beginner to QBasic. In any case, read on, faithful one, because in 27 quick chapters, you'll know QBasic.

What Makes This Book Different?

This book does not cloud issues with internal technical stuff that beginners to QBasic programming don't need. The author (me) is of the firm belief that introductory principles have to be taught well and slowly. After the basics are tackled, the "harder" parts never seem hard. This book teaches you the real QBasic that you need to get started.

QBasic was designed for beginners. If QBasic is the first language you have decided to learn, you picked a winner. QBasic is kind to beginners while providing the commands needed by the experts.

Any subject, whether it be brain surgery, mail sorting, or QBasic programming, is easy if explained properly. Nobody can teach you anything, because you have to teach yourself. But if the instructor, book, or video doing the teaching doesn't make the subject simple and fun, you won't *want* to learn the subject.

I challenge you to find a more straightforward approach to QBasic than is offered in *Absolute Beginner's Guide to QBasic*. If you can, call me, because I'd like to read it too (you thought maybe I'd offer your money back?). Seriously, I have attempted to provide you with a different kind of help from that which you find in most other places.

The biggest advantage *Absolute Beginner's Guide to QBasic* offers is that the author (still me) really *likes* QBasic. Unlike most "computer people," I learned to write BASIC programs (BASIC is the predecessor of QBasic) before I learned anything else. When I first sat down at a computer years ago, it was in front of a BASIC language manual, and I've been hooked ever since. I hope I can help hook you also.

Conventions Used in This Book

The following typographic conventions are used in this book:

 Code lines, variables, and any text you see on-screen are in `monospace` type.

 Placeholders on format lines are in *`italic monospace`*.

Parts of program output that the user typed are in **`bold monospace`**.

 Filenames are in regular text, all uppercase (for example, SLOTS.BAS).

 Optional parameters in syntax explanations are enclosed in flat brackets ([ ]). You do *not* type the brackets when you include these parameters.

 New terms appear in *italic*.

 Some code lines are too long to fit on a single line in the book. A line with the code-continuation character, ➥, has been continued from the preceding line.

Index to the Icons

Like many computer books, this book contains lots of helpful hints, tips, and warnings. You will run across many *icons* (little pictures) that bring these items to your attention. A glance at the icon gives you a quick idea of the purpose of the text next to the icon.

Here are descriptions of the book's icons:

YIKES!

This icon points out potential problems you could face with the particular topic being discussed. Often, the icon indicates a warning that you should heed, or it provides a way to fix a problem that can occur.

PSST!  All of this book's hints and tips (and there are lots of them) are highlighted by this icon. When a really neat feature or code trick coincides with the topic you are reading about, this icon pinpoints just what you can do to take advantage of the bonus.

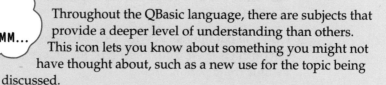

Throughout the QBasic language, there are subjects that provide a deeper level of understanding than others. This icon lets you know about something you might not have thought about, such as a new use for the topic being discussed.

Skip This, It's Technical

If you don't want anything more than the beginning essentials of QBasic, don't read the material next to this icon. Actually, most of you will enjoy this material, but be aware that you can safely skip it without losing the meaning of the chapter.

How Can I Have Fun with QBasic?

Appendix B contains a complete working slot machine program. The program was kept as short as possible without sacrificing readable code and game-playing functionality. After you learn QBasic, you'll easily be able to access QBasic's specific graphics, sound, and input routines to improve the program.

The program uses as much of this book's content as possible. Almost every topic taught in the book appears in the slot machine game. Too many books offer nothing more than snippets of code. The slot machine game in this book gives you the chance to see the *big picture*. As you progress through the book, you'll understand more and more of the game.

What Do I Do Now?

Turn the page and learn the QBasic language.

Part I
ABCs of QBasic

"I need a jeep, canteen, Rhino repellant, machete,
tranquilizer gun, and, oh yes, a computer!"

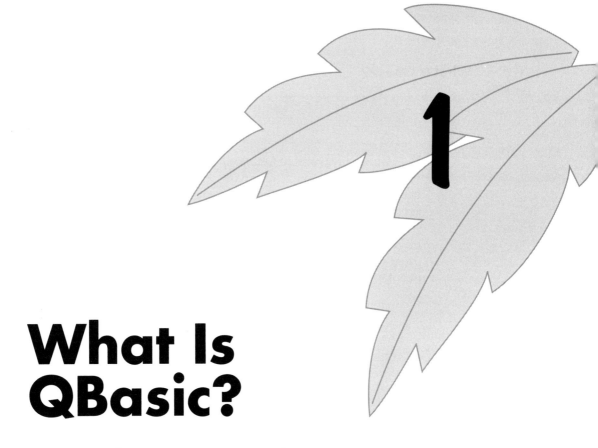

What Is QBasic?

A Fun Programming Language

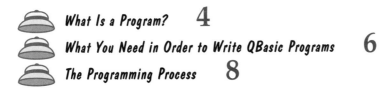

Welcome to the world of QBasic programming! This book will be your guide on the tour through introductory programming. This book shows you that anyone can program computers because programming computers is fun and easy. The programming field seems to never have enough programmers to fill the demand for the programs that have to be written. The tremendous growth in programming jobs seems to have no end in sight. More and more people and businesses are using computers every day.

If you have never written a program in your life, don't worry. This chapter begins at the beginning, teaching you introductory programming concepts, explaining what a program is, and reviewing a short history of the QBasic language. Get ready to be excited! QBasic is a programming language rich in capabilities but easy to master.

What Is a Program?

A computer is nothing more than a dumb machine waiting around for you to give it instructions. When you use a word processor or a spreadsheet, your computer doesn't really know what it's doing. The computer blindly follows instructions without getting bored. Computers do not think or make decisions on their own. Computers must be given extremely detailed instructions before they do anything.

You must supply the detailed instructions when you want your computer to perform a specific task. Those instructions are known as *programs.* A program contains lines of *code,* or instructions that the computer understands. If computers understood English or another spoken language, people wouldn't have to learn to program! Computers cannot, however, understand spoken language. We must meet the computer halfway by supplying instructions in a programming language such as QBasic. The computer then takes those QBasic instructions and translates them into an internal format that is understood by the computer.

Without programs, the computer would just sit idle, not knowing what to do next. A word processing program contains a list of detailed instructions, written in a computer language such as QBasic, that tells the computer exactly how to be a word processor. When you *run* a program, you are telling the computer to follow the instructions in the program that you have supplied.

There are thousands of programs you can buy for your computer, but when a business wants a computer to perform a specific task, the business hires programmers to write programs that follow needed specifications. You will find uses for your computer, but there may not be a program on the market that does what you really want. This book rescues you from that dilemma. After you learn QBasic, you will be able to write programs that contain instructions which tell the computer how to behave.

PSST! A computer program tells your computer how to do what you want. Just as a chef needs a recipe to make a dish, a computer needs instructions to produce results. A recipe is nothing more than a set of detailed instructions that, if properly written, describe the steps needed to prepare a food item. That is exactly what a computer program is to your computer.

Programs produce *output* when you *run* or *execute* them. The cooked dish is a recipe's *output*, and the payroll or word processor is the output produced by a running program. If no output were needed, there would be no need for computers or computer programs. Your computer exists to perform tasks and create output that you need.

Figure 1.1.

Without a program, your computer gathers dust for a living.

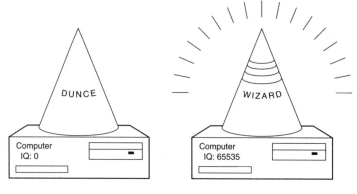

A Computer Without a Program   A Computer With a Program

What You Need in Order to Write QBasic Programs

Before you can write and execute a QBasic program on your computer, you need a QBasic programming language. The QBasic programming language, more accurately known by the computer industry as a QBasic *interpreter,* takes the QBasic program you write, interprets it (which is a technical term for making the program computer-readable), and then runs the program so that you can look at the resulting output. Today's QBasic interpreter is much more advanced than the predecessor BASIC language interpreters of a few years ago.

The QBasic interpreter is supplied free with each version of DOS sold today. Starting with DOS 5.0, Microsoft Corporation (the founding company of QBasic and many other versions of BASIC over the years) wants to provide everybody with the QBasic language so that today's beginners will have a head start toward becoming tomorrow's expert programmers.

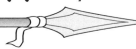

YIKES!

If you are unfamiliar with DOS, have no fear! You don't have to be a DOS wizard to use QBasic.

Microsoft Corporation has been writing versions of the BASIC language for almost 20 years now. In one of the earliest renditions, called *MBASIC* (for *Microsoft BASIC*), Microsoft took a language written for beginners and added powerful features while maintaining the ease of use that beginners need. Over the years, Microsoft made many refinements to BASIC. The result is QBasic, one of the most powerful interpreted languages on the market today, and still one of the cheapest (free!).

Skip This, It's Technical

BASIC began as an alternative to the harder-to-use FORTRAN programming language. Nonprogramming students who needed to write programs for their classes didn't need to fight both their own subject material and a difficult programming language. Therefore, some college professors put their heads together and developed BASIC, which stands for *Beginner's All-Purpose Symbolic Instruction Code*.

PSST! Don't let that long acronym dissuade you! QBasic is easier to use than its silver-dollar abbreviation would lead you to believe. The key word is *Beginner's*.

Microsoft Corporation offers other versions of BASIC, the most notable one being the QuickBASIC *compiler* and Visual BASIC for Windows. (A compiler is a lot like an interpreter but is a little more trouble to use.) Microsoft's Word for Windows word processor and Microsoft Access, a powerful database system, include BASIC-like languages as well. When you master QBasic, you'll be more than ready to tackle these other versions of BASIC.

Skip This, It's Technical

The QBasic program you write is called *source code*. The QBasic interpreter takes QBasic source code and translates the code into *machine language*. Computers are made up of nothing more than thousands of electrical switches that are either *on* or *off*. Computers must ultimately be given instructions in *binary*. The prefix *bi* means two, and the two states of electricity are called *binary states*. It's a lot easier to use the QBasic interpreter to convert your QBasic programs into 1s and 0s that represent internal on and off switch settings than for you to do it yourself.

The Programming Process

Most people follow these basic steps when writing any program:

1. Decide exactly what the program is to do.

2. Use an *editor* to write and save the programming language instructions. An editor is a lot like a word processor (although not usually as fancy) that enables you to create and edit text. All QBasic program filenames end in .BAS.

3. Run the program.

4. Check for program errors. If there are any, fix them and go back to step 3.

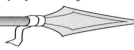

An error in a computer program is called a *bug*.
Getting rid of errors is called *debugging a program.*

QBasic enables you to perform these steps easily, all from within the same environment. For instance, you can use QBasic's editor to enter a program, run the program, view any errors, fix the errors, run the program, and look at the results, all from within the same screen and using a uniform set of menus.

YIKES!

If you have never programmed before, this all might seem confusing. Relax. This book will hold your hand the entire way and challenge you to learn at the same time.

In a nutshell, you really have to take only these steps when writing QBasic programs: Start QBasic, type your program, and press Shift+F5 (one of the keyboard's *function keys*) to run your program. QBasic takes care of interpreting and executing the program.

Fun Fact
The first bug really was a bug! A moth was lodged in an early printer, which lead to the term computer bug.

PSST! Many times, QBasic finds bugs in your programs. If you spell a command incorrectly, for instance, QBasic tells you so when you attempt to run the program.

YIKES!

Put on your thinking caps and set your phasers on QBasic because the next chapter takes you on a journey through the QBasic environment.

Happy Hunting

 Make sure you have a version of DOS that is 5.0 or later.

 Learn the QBasic programming language. This book takes care of that!

Charged

 Don't get nervous, because QBasic programs are easy to write. The QBasic environment has many more features than you will ever have to learn.

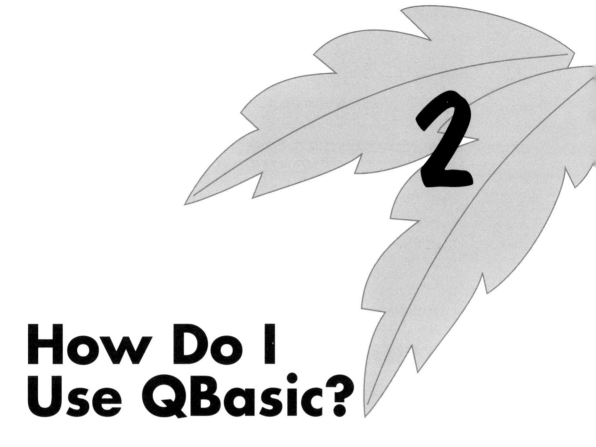

How Do I Use QBasic?

Learn the QBasic Editor

This chapter puts you at ease inside QBasic's environment. You won't learn how to write QBasic programs yet—that begins in the next chapter. You will see here how to start QBasic and how to load from and save programs to the disk.

You cannot physically harm your computer from its keyboard (you can only hurt its feelings…no, just kidding). Therefore, after you load QBasic, play around and try a few things. The only way to learn something like QBasic is to use it.

Starting QBasic

Hopefully your computer has a hard disk. If it does not, the way you start QBasic will be different from the method described here. Even some readers who have hard disks will have trouble loading QBasic because of a nonstandard method that was used to load QBasic and DOS originally. If you have problems, this is one of the few times you'll have to learn a little about DOS or, better yet, ask a friend to help you. Most readers of this book will be able to start QBasic by following these steps:

1.   Turn on the computer if it is not already on.

2.   Find the *DOS prompt,* which usually looks like this:

     `C:\>`

     If you see a letter other than *C* before the `:\>`, that means that a drive other than C is currently active. Do not worry if C is not the active drive because things should still work fine.

3.   Type QBASIC at the DOS prompt. Press ESC (Escape) to get rid of the copyright message box, and you'll see the screen shown in Figure 2.1. The figure also points out a few areas of the screen that we'll need to discuss in this chapter.

Figure 2.1.

Great, you've started QBasic.

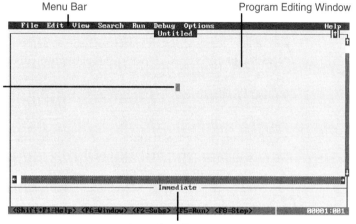

Menu Bar

Program Editing Window

Mouse Cursor

Immediate Execution Window

PSST! If you are running QBasic from Windows, double-click on the QBasic icon in the Main Program Group.

Looking At QBasic's Environment

The large blank area in the middle of the screen is called the *program editing window.* Here you will see your program as you type it, just as you see your text on a word processor's screen as you enter text there.

The *text cursor* marks the location of the current character. As you type, the cursor moves forward. As you edit text, you can move the text cursor up, down, left, and right to change your editing position. If you have a mouse, you will see the *mouse cursor* as well. The mouse cursor enables you to move the text cursor quickly. Instead of using the arrow keys, you can move the mouse cursor and click the left mouse button, and the text cursor will move to wherever the mouse cursor is at the time.

The mouse cursor is useful for selecting, cutting, and pasting blocks of text. You can also use the mouse cursor to click within the horizontal and vertical scroll bars to scroll the screen over different parts of a long program. And you can use the mouse cursor to select from QBasic's wide assortment of menus, which are discussed in a moment.

The status line in the lower-right corner of the screen shows the line and column of the text cursor's current position. (The line number is the five-digit number to the left of the colon, and the column number is to the right of the colon.)

PSST!   Type a few things into QBasic's editing window, and watch the screen as you do so. The line and column numbers will change as you type, and the text cursor will move too. If you have a mouse, move it around and click it a few times as well.

YIKES!

If QBasic displays an error message as you type, press Enter to get rid of the error. For now, it is important that you get familiar with QBasic's editor so that you can give your full concentration to the language later.

Skip This, It's Technical

The *immediate execution window* is handy if you want to try a one-line QBasic statement. You can move the cursor down to this area and type a line of code such as PRINT 20*30 to see the results immediately. The line you type here does not affect the program in the editing window above.

QBasic includes a *menu* bar across the top of the screen with options such as **F**ile, **E**dit, and **V**iew. A menu is a list of options displaying the orders you can issue to QBasic. You can select from any of the menus in one of two ways:

 Press the Alt key, then press the boldfaced letter of the menu option you want to choose.

 If you have a mouse, move the mouse pointer over the option, and click the left mouse button.

The menu you see when you select from the menu bar is called a *pull-down menu* because the menu acts like a rolling window shade that you might pull down. Choose any of the pull-down menu options by moving the highlight bar over the option with the arrow keys and pressing Enter. You can use the mouse to choose an option by moving the mouse cursor so that it points to the option and then clicking the left mouse button.

 Display a menu option by selecting **F**ile. QBasic displays a list of items under **F**ile from which you can choose by pressing the arrow keys and Enter or by clicking with the mouse.

The tear-out card in this book contains a description of QBasic's menu options. Beginning QBasic programmers have little use for most of the menu options on the various pull-down menus.

As you glance through the QBasic pull-down menus, you will notice that some options have keystrokes listed next to them. For instance, the **S**tart option on the **R**un pull-down menu has Shift+F5 listed next to it. Shift+F5 is the *shortcut key* for that option; instead of selecting the option from the menu, you need only press Shift+F5 and QBasic will know that you want to select **S**tart from the **R**un pull-down menu. Pressing Shift+F5 is quicker than selecting from the menu.

Most of the shortcut keys use one of the function keys listed on the side or across the top of your keyboard (the keys labeled F1 through F10 or F12). This book's tear-out card lists all the QBasic shortcut keys.

YIKES!

Do not try to memorize the shortcut keys now—rely on the menus to tell you what you can do next. As you use QBasic, you will learn the shortcut keys.

PSST! Using the shortcut keys is quicker than selecting from the menus, even if you have a mouse. Nevertheless, these keys take some time to learn. As you use QBasic's menus, pay attention to the shortcut keys and learn the ones for the menu options you use most.

Some of the menu options have an ellipsis after them, such as the Display... option from the **O**ptions menu. Instead of performing an action, these menu options produce *dialog boxes.* A dialog box appears when QBasic needs more information to carry out your command. Often, a dialog box requires that you type a program filename to load or save, as the section "Loading Your Work" shows you later in this chapter.

QBasic to the Rescue

When you really need help with QBasic, ask QBasic! QBasic supplies lots of helpful advice that you can use for editing and programming. Although QBasic supplies several kinds of help, most of the time, you'll want help with a particular command.

For instance, type PRINT in the QBasic editing window, and then press F1 (the help shortcut key). QBasic displays a large help screen in place of the editing window describing the ins and outs of the PRINT command. Pressing ESC gets rid of the help screen. The F1 key produces *context-sensitive help,* which is a fancy term meaning that you get help on the command at the cursor's current location.

PSST!   The right mouse button brings up help also.

HMM...   Notice that QBasic restores your editing window when you are through viewing the help screen.

PSST!   Pull down the **Help** menu, and look through some of the other kinds of help that QBasic provides.

Saving Your Work

Save your QBasic program to disk often. If the power goes out (or more likely, some goof walks along and pulls out your power cord from the wall), you will lose any work you haven't saved to disk. Type something into your QBasic editing window (it doesn't have to be an actual program), and select **S**ave from the **File** pull-down menu. Type a filename next to the File **N**ame prompt.

HMM...

The filename must be a valid one- to eight-character DOS filename. All QBasic program files should end in the .BAS filename extension. You don't have to type the .BAS extension because QBasic supplies that for you.

Skip This, It's Technical

If you understand DOS drive and subdirectory names, you can type either one before the filename.

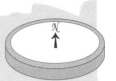

Loading Your Work

If you want to load a program from disk into memory, you can do so through the File pull-down menu. Before loading the program you just saved, select File New. This action erases your program editing window and prepares QBasic for a new program file. (If you don't select File New, QBasic will replace whatever is in the editing window with the loaded file anyway.)

PSST!    You can load only one file at a time into QBasic. If you want to change two or more QBasic programs, you'll have to load and change them one at a time.

Select File Open from the pull-down menus. Type the filename you entered in the preceding section. Again, you don't have to type the .BAS extension because QBasic assumes that all of your QBasic

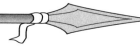

program files end in .BAS. (You can also just select the file from the list of filenames.) You will see the text you entered at the end of the preceding section.

Quitting QBasic

Before you return to the operating system, save your work if you haven't already, and then select **F**ile E**x**it from the pull-down menus. QBasic closes up and you return to DOS.

YIKES!

If you try to leave QBasic before saving your file, QBasic warns you and gives you one last chance to save your program.

PSST! Always return to DOS before powering off your computer. Doing so keeps you from accidentally forgetting to save a program.

Happy Hunting

 Start QBasic and practice entering text.

 Always save your program to disk so that it will be there the next time you want to work on it.

Remember the F1 help key because QBasic's help is there when you need it.

Fun Fact
Early program editors were known as line editors. *Programmers could edit a single line at a time and could not move the cursor up and down the screen as can be done with editors such as QBasic's full-screen editor.*

Charged

 Don't use a strange filename extension. QBasic expects the .BAS filename extension on all your program files.

What's a QBasic Program Like?

The Program's Format

This chapter eases you into QBasic by getting you used to the *big picture*. Before you are done, you'll be able to recognize a QBasic program and understand what is needed to run one. You learned in the preceding chapter that entering a QBasic program takes no more effort than entering text into a word processor. A program is nothing more than lines of instructions that you type. Many of QBasic's commands look just like their English equivalents, such as PRINT, IF, and WHILE.

The Forest Without the Trees

A complete QBasic program follows this paragraph. The program is short; QBasic programs don't have to be mammoth to be useful. Glance through the code. At this point, you don't have to understand any of the individual lines. Familiarize yourself with the program's look and feel.

```
REM Introductory program
REM This program prints your name across the screen.
CLS
INPUT "What is your first name"; firstName$
CLS
FOR row = 1 TO 24 STEP 2
   FOR col = 1 TO 70 STEP 5
      LOCATE row, col          ' Move the cursor
      PRINT firstName$
      FOR tmr = 1 TO 500       ' Timing loop
      NEXT tmr
      LOCATE row, col
      PRINT STRING$(LEN(firstName$), " ");
   NEXT col
   BEEP       ' Beep the speaker at the end of each row
NEXT row
END
```

QBasic programs are *free-form*. That is, you are free to insert extra lines and spaces just about anywhere you want. The indention of the middle lines of code is not needed, but after you learn more about QBasic, you'll see why this indention helps the readability of the program.

YIKES!

If you want to type this program and run it, feel free to. Doing so will be good practice. However, be sure to type the program *exactly* as you see it. Although QBasic is gentle to new programmers, it can be grumpy at times, especially with typing errors.

If you want to enter this program and run it, you can run the program in one of two ways: by selecting **R**un **S**tart from the menu or by pressing Shift+F5, which is the shortcut key for **R**un **S**tart. This is how you run any QBasic program, from the shortest to the longest.

If you get an error message, such as the one shown in Figure 3.1, you typed something incorrectly. Press OK at the error message prompt and correct the problem. If you select Help at the error message, QBasic displays some advice on why you got the error. Most of the time, you probably misspelled a name somewhere.

PSST! QBasic tries to help you all it can. When QBasic encounters an error, it tries to place the text cursor on the line where the error probably happened.

When a program finishes, QBasic does not hurry back to the editing screen. Instead, QBasic displays the following message at the bottom of the screen:

```
Press any key to continue
```

When you press a key, the QBasic editing window returns. The message gives you a chance to look at the last part of whatever program you just ran. If QBasic raced back to the editing window when it was through, you would miss what was on-screen at the end of the program's execution.

Figure 3.1.

Oops! An error needs attention.

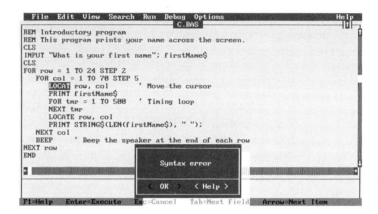

PSST!   When you're back at the editing window, you can always peek back at the program's output by pressing F4, the shortcut key for **V**iew **O**utput Screen.

After you type the program and run it, save it to your disk. After reading a few chapters in this book, you might want to reload this program and study it to see how it works.

Looking At a Longer Program

Microsoft supplies several programs with QBasic. A couple of them, GORILLA.BAS and NIBBLES.BAS, are games you can play. As a matter of fact, this might be a good time to load and take a look at a

lengthy QBasic program. To load the GORILLA.BAS program, follow these steps:

1. Select **File Open** from the menu bar.

2. At the File **Name** prompt, type `C:\DOS\GORILLA.BAS` and then press Enter. After a brief pause, you'll see the message `Q B a s i c    G o r i l l a s` at the top of the editing window.

YIKES!

If you get a `File not found` error message, either someone deleted the GORILLA.BAS file or DOS is not installed on the C: drive in the directory named DOS. You might have to get help in finding the file if you are unfamiliar with DOS commands and directories.

3. Press Shift+F5 to run the program. (Remember that Shift+F5 is the shortcut key for **Run Start**.)

4. Don't monkey around too much! You've got a programming language to learn!

PSST!   If you want to quit in the middle of a QBasic program's execution, press Ctrl+Break. When QBasic senses a Ctrl+Break keystroke, control is given back to you in the editing window.

Scanning a Long Program

The GORILLA.BAS program is a long one. In fact, it gives you a good chance to search through a program that takes more than a single screen. When a program is longer than one screen, your computer's screen acts like a camera that scans up and down a viewing area. Because you can view only 20 or so lines at a time, you can use the arrow keys, PageUp, and PageDown to move your computer screen through the long program.

HMM... The GORILLA.BAS game is a graphics-oriented game. If you have a monochrome text adapter and monitor, you'll get this error message when you attempt to run the program:

```
Sorry, you must have CGA, EGA color, or VGA graphics to play
➥GORILLA.BAS
```

The scroll bar on the right side of the screen is handy for mouse users as well. You can scroll through a long program by clicking on the scroll bar or moving the scroll bar's *elevator box* up and down by dragging it with a mouse.

YIKES!

Five years ago who would have thought that we would be saying something like "Move the elevator up and down by dragging it with a mouse" and not think a thing about it?!

Printing a Program Listing

Often, you'll want to print a program's listing to paper. Doing so gives you an easier way to view more of the program at once. During debugging sessions of long programs, sometimes the screen size just won't give you enough room to find a problem in the code.

To print a program, follow the steps given next. (If you have the GORILLA.BAS program still loaded, it takes about 20 pages to print. You might want to load a shorter program, such as the one from the beginning of this chapter, to save paper.)

1. Turn on your printer and make sure it has paper.

2. Select **File Print** from the menu bar. QBasic displays a box in the middle of the screen.

3. Most of the time, you'll want the entire program to print, so press Enter. This selects Entire Program from the box on the screen (the *default* selection). If you wanted to print only part of a program, you could move the dot up or down to the other two options with the arrow keys or the mouse.

Happy Hunting

 Type the program listed in this chapter and run it for practice.

 Use the scroll bars, arrow keys, and PageUp and PageDown keys to move through a long program.

 Press Ctrl+Break when you want to quit a program before its natural conclusion.

Charged

 Don't worry about any individual program statements at this point. The next chapter begins exploring QBasic programming statements in detail.

 Don't try the two QBasic games if you don't have a graphics card and monitor. GORILLA.BAS and NIBBLES.BAS are designed for PCs with graphics adapters.

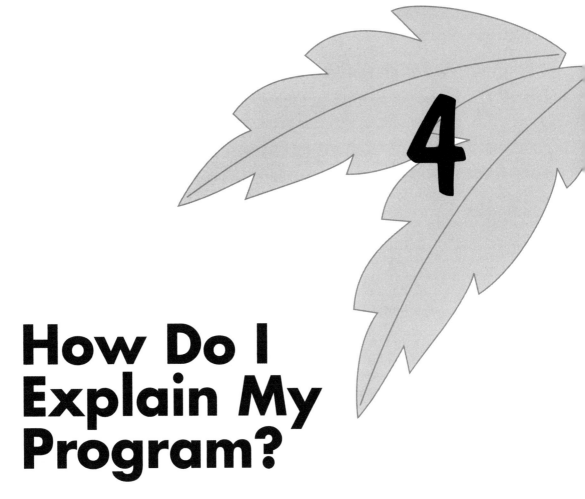

How Do I Explain My Program?

With Remarks

You write programs for computers, but people also read your programs. Companies that hire programmers understand the need for *readable* programs—readable not just for computers but also for people. Companies' needs change and so do the programs that companies use. Throughout this book, you will learn ways to improve the readability of your code so that you can be in demand as a programmer who writes readable code.

It has been said that a program is written once but read a thousand times. Although such a statement seems better suited in a book of proverbs, it has a lot of truth in the world of computers. The code you write must be clear so that you can easily change it in the future if the need arises. More important for the company you program for, your programs must be readable so that whoever is assigned to change your program later will be able to.

This chapter teaches you the most important part of writing readable programs. It is here that you'll learn how to add *remarks* to the programs you write.

REMarkable Documentation

Remarks are messages that explain what is happening in the program. Remarks are not for the computer; remarks are for people. Your remarks are completely ignored by QBasic, and yet they are some of the most important QBasic statements you will learn.

If you write a program that manages an inventory system, the remarks will explain how the inventory total calculations work, how the data must be formatted for input into files, and how the inventory listings get printed.

HMM... What if you don't program for a living, but write programs on your own for fun and profit? You don't really need remarks, right? Well, not exactly. You never know when you might have to change a program you wrote. Instead of filtering through a lot of QBasic code, you can more easily scan through remarks looking for the section that needs changing.

PSST! Good habits are best learned early. Add remarks *as* you write your programs. Get in the habit now because programmers rarely go back and add remarks after the code is written.

Consider the following QBasic statement:

```
IF LEFT$(UCASE$(C$), 1) = "Y" THEN
```

This statement takes a little study, even for veteran QBasic programmers. An added short remark, however, explains the statement nicely:

```
IF LEFT$(UCASE$(C$), 1) = "Y" THEN   ' See if the user typed a Y
```

The next few sections describe how to add remarks, but even without explanation you can probably figure out that the text to the right of the apostrophe, ', is a remark. You can add as many blank spaces after a line of code and before the apostrophe as you want in order to make the statement and remark readable.

Because remarks are for people and not computers, don't add remarks just for the sake of adding them. Your remarks should explain to people what is going on. Consider this statement:

```
LET al = 21          ' Make al equal to 21
```

This remark is redundant (which is fancy lingo for *really stupid and unneeded*). The remark explains nothing about the statement. The remark is little more than a rewrite of the QBasic code next to it. Consider this change:

```
LET al = 21          ' Save the age limit for future comparisons
```

Ah, now *that's* a remark! The remark truly explains what is being done by the code on the left. Remember that remarks are for people (including you) looking at your programs, not for computers, as Figure 4.1 illustrates. The computer doesn't need remarks! The computer understands QBasic without them.

Figure 4.1.

Friends don't let friends write programs without remarks.

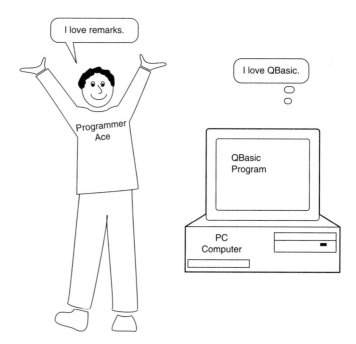

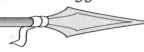

PSST! Don't overdo remarks. Not every QBasic statement needs a remark. Add remarks only if they clarify what the code is doing. The following statement probably needs no remark:

```
PRINT "Hello"
```

Whether you know QBasic or not, you can tell that the statement prints the word Hello on-screen. A remark telling you that would add nothing.

HMM... There might be times in this book when a statement is over-remarked. You are just learning to program, and an extra remark here and there rarely hurts because you are just getting familiar with the QBasic commands.

Adding Remarks

Remarks can be specified in one of two ways: either by the REM statement or by a single apostrophe, ', as you saw earlier. Here is a section of code with REM statements:

```
REM The next few lines will calculate gross pay
REM then calculate the taxes so that net pay
REM then can be found.
GP = rate * hours
Taxes = GP * .35
NP = GP - Taxes
```

When you specify a remark with REM, everything following REM on that line is a remark, and QBasic knows to completely ignore the line. Anything can follow REM because people, not the computer, read the remarks. You don't have to worry about exact placement of anything after REM. Just be sure the remark makes sense and describes the code well.

The apostrophe remarks have the advantage of being able to reside on lines by themselves in addition to being able to follow QBasic statements on the same line. Here is a rewritten version of the section of code using both REM and the apostrophes:

```
REM The next few lines calculate payroll figures
GP = rate * hours    ' Gross pay calculation
Taxes = GP * .35     ' Compute taxes
NP = GP - Taxes      ' Net pay results
```

YIKES!

Don't worry about which remark is the best. There is no best. The apostrophe is used more because of its flexibility, but use whichever you feel most comfortable with.

HMM...

The slot machine game in Appendix B contains lots of remarks. Look through the program and read its remarks. Even though you know no QBasic so far, you can get an idea of how the program works just from reading the remarks.

If you write programs for a living, you should know that many companies require that their programmers place their own names at the top of programs, inside remarks, including the date the programmer wrote the program. If the program later needs to be changed, the original programmer can be found to answer questions or help with the changes. Often, programmers put the program's filename in a remark at the top of the program as well.

Here is a complete QBasic program that includes lots of remarks for your perusal:

```
REM Filename: PAYAVG.BAS
REM Written by Pauline Programmer on July 4, 1995
REM
' This program asks users for their previous three salary
' figures, then averages the salaries.
INPUT "What was your salary three years ago"; sal1
INPUT "What was your salary two years ago"; sal2
INPUT "What was your salary last year"; sal3
avg = (sal1 + sal2 + sal3) / 3     ' Computes the average
PRINT
PRINT "The average for the three years is"; avg
END
```

PSST!   Always end your QBasic programs with an END statement. END marks the end of the program listing and its execution. QBasic doesn't require END, but an END statement indicates to anyone looking at your program exactly where the end is.

Happy Hunting

 Use remarks abundantly throughout all your programs. When in doubt, add a remark.

 QBasic remarks begin with REM or '. Use the ' for more flexibility.

Charged

 Don't overdo remarks. Redundant remarks are no more useful than no remarks.

In Review

The goal of this chapter is to teach you the importance of commenting your code with remarks. Remarks are for people looking at your program, not for QBasic. There are two ways to begin a comment: with REM or with the apostrophe, '.

QBasic ignores everything that follows a remark. Therefore, you would never want to put QBasic commands to the right of a remark. Many programmers put their own names in a remark statement at the top of the program to document the program's author in case there are questions later.

Code Example

Here are two lines without remarks:

```
FOR i = 1 TO 100 STEP 5
f$ = LEFT$(full$, fNum)
```

And here are the same two statements with remarks:

```
FOR i = 1 TO 100 STEP 5     ' Count by 5s from 1 to 100
REM The next statement assigns a person's first name to
REM the variable f$.
f$ = LEFT$(full$, fNum)
```

Code Analysis

You can see how the remarks help document what is going on with the QBasic statements. A nonprogrammer ought to be able to look at your remarks and have a good idea of what is going on with the code.

Part II
Early QBasic Programming

"I say, old chap! Have you seen my mouse?"

Can I Write Simple Programs Yet?

Yes, with **PRINT**

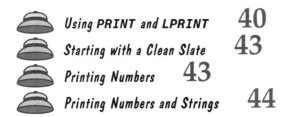

The command perhaps used most in QBasic programs is PRINT. The PRINT command produces output on your screen. When you sit down to use a computer, don't you read the screen a lot? The programs you run must constantly output stuff to the screen so that the user will know what is happening. If a payroll program computed payroll figures but never printed them, the program wouldn't be worth a lot to anybody.

This chapter explains how to write simple programs that produce output. The output is sent not only to the screen but, using the PRINT command's cousin, the LPRINT command, to the printer as well.

Using PRINT and LPRINT

PRINT has lots of formats. Even veteran QBasic programmers don't always know every format of PRINT, but that's OK. You need to know only a little about PRINT to make it handle most of your output needs. As stated in the introduction, PRINT sends stuff (letters, words, numbers, sentences, whatever) to the screen. PRINT is known as an *output* statement because it takes the output that your program produces and displays that output for the user of the program to see. Figure 5.1 explains what PRINT (and its cousin LPRINT) is all about.

HMM...

You'll use PRINT for virtually anything that appears on the computer's screen. There are other ways to produce screen output, but using PRINT is the most common.

The easiest thing to print is a *string*. A QBasic string is nothing more than zero or more characters enclosed in quotation marks. Both of these are strings:

```
"QBasic is fun!"
"448-65-0900"
```

Figure 5.1.

PRINT and LPRINT produce output from QBasic programs.

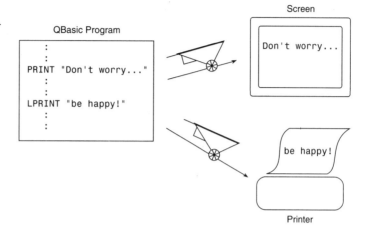

Skip This, It's Technical

You can indicate an empty string, called a *null string,* by placing two quotation marks next to each other like this: " ". Sometimes the null string comes in handy for initializing strings that you don't yet have data for.

PSST! Notice that strings can contain numbers as well as characters. If you have to work with a group of digits, such as a phone number, Social Security number, or ZIP code, and you are *not* going to do math with the number, keep it as a string. Later in this chapter, you'll see how to specify numbers that aren't strings.

Here is the format for printing strings:

```
PRINT string
```

YIKES!

Throughout this book, when you see a new use for a command, you'll first be given the command's format. Anything in italics means that something else goes there, in this case the *string* of your choice. Words that aren't in italics, like PRINT, are required.

For example, when your QBasic program encounters the line

```
PRINT "QBasic is easy!"
```

the words QBasic is easy! appear on-screen. Type the following short program into QBasic and select **Run Start** to see the results. (If there is already a program in your QBasic editor, save it if you want to keep it, or select **File New** to erase it before entering this program.)

```
REM Program to print some strings
PRINT "My QBasic programs are so much fun"
PRINT "I think I'd like to see them run."
PRINT "I'll type the statements one by one"
PRINT "and be so glad when I am done."
END
```

Notice that each PRINT's output begins on a new line when you run the program. You'll later learn how to keep PRINT statements from starting new lines.

Starting with a Clean Slate

If you entered and ran the preceding program, it should have worked fine, but there is a slight problem with the output. Whatever was on the output screen before you ran the program will still be there above the output of your program. It would be nice to erase the output screen completely before your program runs so that each program produces its own output on a clear screen.

QBasic supplies the CLS (for *clear screen*) command to do just that. When QBasic encounters CLS, your output screen is erased before anything is printed. Therefore, add the following statement to the top of the program just entered, and rerun the program:

```
CLS          ' Erase the screen
```

Isn't the program's output easier to read when you clear the screen first?

There is one more item related to clearing the screen. If you use PRINT on a line by itself, QBasic prints a blank line. In the following short program, QBasic clears the screen, prints Hello, prints a blank line, and then prints Good-bye.

```
CLS
PRINT "Hello"
PRINT                     ' Blank line is printed
PRINT "Good-bye"
END
```

Printing Numbers

Printing numbers is just as easy as printing strings. As a matter of fact, some people would argue that numbers are easier because you don't have to enclose numbers in quotation marks. If you want to print the numbers from 1 to 3, here is how you can do it:

```
PRINT 1
PRINT 2
PRINT 3
```

Of course, you could have enclosed the numbers in quotation marks and QBasic would have still printed the numbers from 1 to 3 on separate lines.

YIKES!

QBasic always prints a space before and after positive numbers. Therefore, the 1, 2, and 3 would print with a space before them (the space wouldn't be there if you enclosed the numbers in quotation marks). QBasic prints a negative sign (and no space) before negative numbers.

Printing Numbers and Strings

Don't have your QBasic programs print numbers on the screen or printer without accompanying messages that tell what the numbers mean. For example, if you wanted to tell the user to enter three values, which is clearer? This:

```
3
```

Or this:

```
You must enter 3 values.
```

Obviously, describing your numeric output is best.

Any time you want to print more than one value on a single line, whether those values are strings, numbers, or a combination of both, separate each item with a semicolon, ;. For example, you can print the preceding line like this:

```
PRINT "You must enter"; 3; "values."
```

Of course, you could have enclosed the entire line in quotation marks and you wouldn't have to use the semicolon. However, you need to understand the separating semicolon so that you'll understand how to output the data described in the next chapter.

PSST! If you put a trailing semicolon at the end of a PRINT statement, a subsequent PRINT output will not appear on the next line. The following two PRINT statements print both words on one line because of the first PRINT's trailing semicolon:

```
PRINT "Miami, ";
PRINT "Florida"
```

Happy Hunting

 Use the PRINT statement to send output to the screen.

 Use the LPRINT statement to send output to the printer.

 Use the CLS command to erase the screen.

Charged

 Don't forget to enclose all string data in quotation marks.

 Don't print numbers without some kind of descriptive string.

In Review

The goal of this chapter is to teach you how to send output to your screen or printer from your QBasic program. The PRINT command sends output to the screen, and the LPRINT command sends output to the printer.

PRINT is one of the most common QBasic commands and is used in almost every program. After all, most programs write to the screen. You can print text by enclosing it in quotation marks and print numbers by listing them to the right of PRINT and LPRINT.

Code Example

```
REM The following output statements can go to the printer
REM if you add an L to each of the PRINT statements.
PRINT "This is the first line printed in the program."
PRINT                   ' Prints a blank line
PRINT "I'll now print some numbers:"
PRINT 10
PRINT 20
PRINT 30
PRINT "That's a big"; 10; "-"; 4
END
```

Code Analysis

The program prints a string, a blank line, another string, then three numbers on-screen. Each of these output values appears on a different line of output.

The last line of output prints two strings with two embedded numbers between them. The semicolon outputs values on the same line next to each other. The last line produces this output:

```
That's a big 10 - 4
```

The space appears on either side of the dash because QBasic always leaves a space before and after positive numbers.

How Do I Store Stuff?

Using Variables!

QBasic must have a way to store numbers and strings. If you have ever worked with a calculator that had a memory, you know that the memory enables you to store values so that you can retrieve them later. It is much easier to use the memory than to find a pencil and write down the result that you'll need later. The memory also keeps you from having to calculate the same formula more than once.

QBasic uses *variables* to store data. A variable is a place in memory that you attach a name to in your program. When you store something in a variable, you can later retrieve the value by using the variable name.

PSST!  The word *data* is actually plural for *datum*. Who uses *datum* anymore? We'll stick to the more commonly used *data* for both single and multiple values.

Variables Everywhere

A QBasic program might use many variables. The number of variables you need depends on the application you are programming. If you have lots of different values to track, such as if you're performing a scientific experiment that requires hundreds of calculations, you might need hundreds of variables to hold the results. If you are writing a simple averaging program or writing a program to keep track of a phone list in a disk file, you might not need many variables.

There is no practical limit as to how many variables you can have in a single program. QBasic enables you to have as many as you need. When you need a new variable, you just refer to it by a different name. Therefore, this chapter will explain how to name variables

(because you are responsible for that), how to store data in variables, and how to use variables in your programs.

Think of variables as acting like boxes inside your computer. The variables to your computer are a lot like post office boxes inside a post office. Each post office box has a unique number; each variable has a unique name. No two variables can have the same name.

If two or more variables could have the same name, how would QBasic know which one you wanted to use when you used the name?

There are many types of QBasic variables, and this book will explain each one as we go along. However, these are the two primary kinds of variables:

 Numeric

 String

 PSST! This is easy: Numeric variables hold numbers, and string variables hold strings.

Variables hold data that can change. In the previous program, you saw how to print *constant* data. When you see

```
PRINT 25
```

you know that a 25 prints no matter how many times you run the program. The 25 is known as a *constant* because it remains constant. Variables hold data, such as salary figures, ages, amounts, totals, and other values that can change during a program's execution.

Naming Variables

Learn how to name variables, because *you* are responsible for the names. That is, when you need a variable, you have to assign a unique name to the variable. QBasic variable names can range from 1 to 40 characters, and they must begin with a letter of the alphabet. After the letter, a variable can contain numbers or letters. All the following examples are valid variable names:

```
sales94    Amount    AGE    qtr4Pay93    i
```

It does not matter whether you use uppercase or lowercase letters. You must, however, be consistent. If you first call a variable `Amount`, don't call it `aMOUNT` later, or QBasic will think you renamed the variable and will change the first one you entered to the most recent case.

PSST! Give your variables meaningful names. If you want to store your friend's age, `friendAge` is a much better name than `x12ERddss`, even though QBasic doesn't care which you use.

YIKES!

Don't give a variable the same name as a QBasic command. For instance, QBasic will not enable you to name a variable `END` or `CLS`.

Everything just said about variable names holds for *numeric variables only*. If you want to store a string in a variable, the string variable name must end in a dollar sign, $. Therefore, partNo can hold numbers, but partNo$ can be assigned only strings (either string constants enclosed in quotation marks or other string variables).

Putting Stuff in Variables

Before you put anything into a variable, QBasic puts a zero in the variable for you. You can put something else in the variable with an *assignment* statement. Here is the format of the assignment statement:

```
[LET] variableName = expression
```

YIKES!

Don't actually type the square brackets. When you see square brackets in command formats, the brackets indicate optional keywords. You don't have to type LET when you put values into variables.

Here is how you would store a different number in two variables named Amt1 and Amt2:

```
Amt1 = 2932        ' Stores 2932 into Amt1
Amt2 = 9485        ' Stores 9485 into Amt2
```

You can use the four simple math operators seen in Table 6.1 to store results of calculations in variables.

Table 6.1. **The four QBasic math operators.**

Operator	Description
+	Addition
–	Subtraction
*	Multiplication
/	Division

The following statement puts a 15 in the variable named age:

```
age = 10 + 5
```

PSST! The LET is optional, so many programmers don't type it. The following assignment is exactly the same as the previous statement:

```
LET age = 10 + 5
```

A calculation can even contain other variables. Consider the following example:

```
sales = 39456.54
costOfSales = 10233.90
netSales = sales - costOfSales
```

The variable named netSales contains the difference between the total sales and the cost of sales. (See how meaningful variable names make the code clearer?)

Here's some code that stores two names in two string variables:

```
company1$ = "Kranco, Inc."
company2$ = "Super Amalgamated"
```

You know that company1$ and company2$ can hold only strings because their names end with a dollar sign.

Study Figure 6.1 to see how these assignment statements store data in memory:

```
age = 46
myName$ = "Terrie"
total = 6 + 7
```

Figure 6.1.

All variables have names and values. The assignment statement stores values in variables.

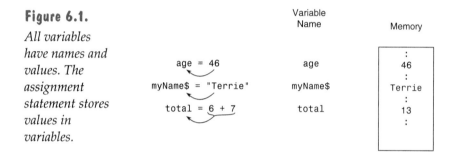

Printing Values in Variables

QBasic makes it easy to print values stored in variables. Just follow a PRINT with the variable name. PRINT will not print the variable names themselves. To show you how PRINT operates, the following PRINT statements produce the output shown after them.

```
a = 10 * 20
b = 6.8 / 2
n$ = "Tony"
PRINT a
PRINT "The value of b is"; b
PRINT n$
PRINT "The value of n$ is "; n$

 200
The value of b is 3.4
Tony
The value of n$ is Tony
```

Happy Hunting

 Use variables to hold data that can change.

 Learn the variable naming rules so that you can assign meaningful names to the variables you use.

 Print variables by specifying their names after PRINT.

 Use the math operators to assign calculated results to variables.

Charged

 Don't give two different variables the same name.

 Don't use a command name for the name of a variable.

In Review

The goal of this chapter is to show you how data is stored in QBasic programs. You don't always know every value needed in a program at the time you write a program. Often, you need to store values and later change them (just as you might do in a more limited fashion on a calculator with several memory storage buttons).

Variables are the holders of a program's data. You store data in a variable by using the equal sign, =. Variables can hold numbers and string data. Before you can use a variable, you must think up a name for the variable that matches the variable naming rules. If you like, you can use the QBasic math operators to calculate values to put in variables.

Code Example

```
REM This program stores and computes several variables
REM before printing them to the screen.
i = 8
j = 10
k = 20
n = i + j + k
x = i * j * k
word$ = "QBasic"
PRINT "The value of i + j + k is"; n
PRINT "The value of i * j * k is"; x
PRINT "The value of word$ is "; word$
END
```

Code Analysis

This program first assigns three numbers to three numeric variables, i, j, and k. A fourth variable, n, holds the sum of the three variables, and a fifth variable, x, holds the product of the three variables.

A string variable is then assigned the string QBasic. A dollar sign has to follow all string variable names. A variable name without a dollar sign is a numeric variable (until you learn how to use more advanced variable-definition commands, discussed in Part V of this book).

If you print a variable using its name, as done in the last three PRINT statements, the value of the variable, not the variable name, goes to the screen.

Can I Ask the User Questions?

Yes, with INPUT

This chapter picks up where the preceding one left off. Chapter 6 showed you how to produce output on the screen and printer. This chapter shows you how to get data from the keyboard (called *input*). A program must be able to receive input from the user sitting at the keyboard. Suppose you were writing a program that calculated daily sales totals for a candy store. At the time you write the program, you have no idea how much candy will be sold. Instead, the program will have to find out each day exactly how much was sold.

The INPUT command accepts keyboard data. When you get to a place in a program that requires keyboard entry, use the INPUT command. There are several formats of INPUT, and this chapter explains the most common ones.

Looking At INPUT

The INPUT command does the opposite job of PRINT. As Figure 7.1 shows, INPUT receives data from the keyboard and stores that data in variables. Before getting data with INPUT, your program should tell the user exactly what kind of data value is expected.

Figure 7.1.

INPUT stores what the user enters into variables.

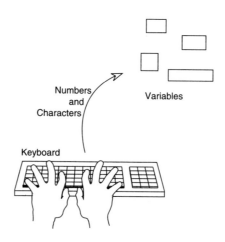

Numbers and Characters

Variables

Keyboard

PSST!   INPUT gets numbers, characters, or strings into variables.

INPUT has several formats. Here is the easiest:

```
INPUT variableName
```

The `variableName` can be any valid QBasic variable. Both of the following examples are valid INPUT commands. The first one inputs a number from the keyboard, and the second one inputs a string.

```
INPUT amt
INPUT lastName$
```

When QBasic encounters INPUT, a question mark (?) appears on the screen, and the program waits for the user to enter a value. INPUT knows when the user is done because the user has to press Enter after typing the input value.

Programmers often print a *prompt* before an INPUT. A prompt is just a message that explains what the INPUT is looking for. For example, if you wanted the user to enter his or her age, your program might contain these two statements:

```
PRINT "What is your age"
INPUT age
```

Because INPUT always produces a question mark, you do not need to put a question mark inside the prompt. However, in the preceding pair of statements, the question mark appears on the line following the prompt, like this:

```
What is your age
?
```

Fun Fact

Before computer keyboards and video screens, all input had to be entered through punched cards and ticker-tape devices! (This was back in ancient times when archaic writing tools called typewriters were still in use.)

You learned in the preceding chapter how to fix this problem. Remember how the trailing semicolon works? A trailing semicolon keeps the cursor from moving down to the next line after a PRINT. Here is a better way to ask for the age:

```
PRINT "What is your age";    ' Suppress the cursor movement
INPUT age
```

When the computer gets to this PRINT, the user sees this:

```
What is your age?
```

When the user types a number, followed by the Enter keystroke, that number is stored in the age variable, and the program then continues.

The following program asks the user for the preceding three days' temperature readings. The average for those three temperatures is computed and printed.

```
' Program that produces a running average of
' the previous 3-day temperature readings.
CLS
PRINT "What is the first day's temperature";
INPUT day1
PRINT "What is the second day's temperature";
INPUT day2
PRINT "What is the third day's temperature";
INPUT day3
' Calculate and print the average
avg = (day1 + day2 + day3) / 3
PRINT                ' Prints a blank line
PRINT "The average temperature was"; avg
END
```

PSST! If the user runs the program several times, entering different values, the program prints a different answer each time. Therefore, with INPUT, you now have programs that respond to changing conditions without requiring rewriting of the code itself.

Here is a sample run from this program:

```
What is the first day's temperature? 87.5
What is the second day's temperature? 92.6
What is the third day's temperature? 90.1

The average temperature was 90.06667
```

HMM... In the preceding example, the average value printed with five decimal places. In Chapter 8, "How Do I Spruce Up My Output?" you'll see how to limit the number of decimal places printed.

Mixing the Prompt with INPUT

QBasic enables you to combine the prompt directly inside the INPUT statement itself. Therefore, instead of using the PRINT-INPUT combination every time you need to get input, you need only use INPUT. Here is the format of the expanded INPUT:

```
INPUT "Prompt message"; variableName
```

An example is worth a thousand words of description. Both of the following sets of code are the same:

```
PRINT "What is your name";
INPUT name$
```

and

```
INPUT "What is your name"; name$
```

YIKES!

Why would you ever want to type two lines when a single one will do the same thing? You wouldn't.

When your computer reaches the INPUT, the user sees this:

```
What is your name?
```

The value the user then types will go into the name$ variable.

Another INPUT Option

There is one more thing you should know about INPUT. If you follow the INPUT prompt with a comma rather than a semicolon, QBasic does not print a question mark. There could be times when you want to prompt the user with something other than a question. For instance, the following INPUT does not automatically display a question mark:

```
INPUT "Please type your answer and press Enter when done...", ans
```

When QBasic gets to this INPUT, the user sees this:

```
Please type your answer and press Enter when done...
```

PSST!   The first two occurrences of INPUT in Appendix B's slot machine game suppress the question mark.

Happy Hunting

 Use INPUT to request values from the user.

 Remember that INPUT always displays a question mark unless you suppress the question mark by using a comma after the prompt.

Charged

 Don't ask for a value unless you prompt the user first. The prompt lets the user know exactly what is expected.

In Review

The goal of this chapter is to teach you how to get input from the user sitting at the keyboard. The user is anyone (including you) who runs the programs that you or somebody else writes.

Use INPUT to accept keyboard input into variables. INPUT displays a question mark unless you suppress the question mark by putting a comma before the INPUT variable name.

Always prompt the user by printing a message indicating what kind of input you want from the user. If a question mark appears out of the blue when a user runs your program, the user has no idea what you are asking for if you don't print a prompt first.

Code Example

```
REM A program that demonstrates several versions of INPUT
PRINT "What is your name";
INPUT nam$
INPUT "What is your age"; age
INPUT iq
INPUT "Hurry, type the result of 5 * 9: ", ans
PRINT
PRINT "Your name is "; nam$
PRINT "You are"; age; "years old."
PRINT "Your IQ is"; iq
PRINT "You said that 5 * 9 is"; ans
END
```

Code Analysis

The program demonstrates the different methods, some good and some not as good, that you can use to get input from the user sitting at the keyboard.

The first INPUT is preceded by a PRINT that asks the user a question. The second INPUT statement shows how to eliminate the PRINT statement. INPUT is capable of displaying a prompt without a separate PRINT statement.

The third INPUT is the most poorly designed one in the program. The user is supposed to type his or her IQ, but the user has no idea what is being asked for. Without a prompting message, the user could type anything regardless of his or her IQ.

The final INPUT suppresses the INPUT statement's question mark by preceding the input variable with a comma.

The values input by the user are then printed with appropriate descriptions before them.

8

How Do I Spruce Up My Output?

With **PRINT** Formatting

There is much more you can do with PRINT and LPRINT. For starters, if you have a color monitor, you might want to output color text rather than drab white on black. After you add color, you can improve your output even more by printing data in columns and formatting your numbers so that they look exactly the way you want them to look.

Anything you can do to improve the look of your program's output helps put the user at ease. Nobody likes to see dollar and cent values printed to four decimal places. Also, anybody sitting in front of a computer using your program all day will appreciate reading color screens. Adding a beep before printing an error message will really wake your user, especially if you print the error in color! This chapter explains how to do both.

Add Flair with Color

If you are writing programs for someone with a color monitor and color graphics adapter (a large percentage of computer users today have both), you can add pizzazz to your programs by coloring the output. The COLOR command enables you to determine exactly what colors your output will appear in. Here is the format of COLOR:

```
COLOR [foreground#] [, background#]
```

The tear-out card in this book lists all of QBasic's colors and the numbers that go with the colors. To specify a color, you must use its number in the COLOR statement. The *foreground* color is the color of the text, and the *background* color is the color of the background screen.

PSST!   In this book, the white page is the background and the black ink is the foreground.

As the format suggests, both the foreground and the background colors are optional—you have to specify only one of them. If you specify only a foreground color number, the background is left unchanged. If you specify only a background color number (the comma indicates that the value is background and not foreground), the foreground remains unchanged.

To print the message This is colorful in white text on a blue background, you can use these lines:

```
COLOR 15, 1    ' Bright white on a blue background
PRINT "This is colorful"
```

After you specify colors with a COLOR statement, all subsequent PRINTs will produce text in that color. Any output that was printed before the COLOR statement remains unchanged.

If you wanted to print bright yellow lettering on the blue background just generated, you could use these lines:

```
COLOR 14      ' Bright yellow foreground
PRINT "This is yellow text still on blue"
```

To change the background to red, you could use these lines:

```
COLOR , 4     ' Notice the comma
PRINT "Yellow on red"
```

As you can see, COLOR affects only *future* printing. If you want the entire screen to become the color you request, follow COLOR with a CLS, like this:

```
COLOR 10, 7   ' Green letters on a white background
CLS           ' Clear the entire screen and give it a
              ' white background
PRINT "This is green on white"
```

YIKES!

Don't overdo colors! Too many colors make your screens look "busy," and your user will more easily tire of the program.

Skip This, It's Technical

If you add 16 to the foreground color, QBasic causes your output to blink on and off. Warning messages such as `Be sure the printer has paper!` might get more attention if you print them in blinking letters.

Line Up: Printing in Columns

If you want output to appear in a specific column, use the `TAB()` function. `TAB()` is called a *function* and not a *command*, but the difference at this point is minor. Use `TAB()` with `PRINT` and `LPRINT`. If you want to print tables of output, you might want to stick tabs between your printed output to force the output to appear in certain columns.

HMM...   Back in prehistoric times, people used typewriters. As you probably know, with typewriters you can set tab stops. QBasic's `TAB()` function works like the typewriter's tab stop.

Here is the format of `TAB()`:

```
TAB(value)
```

You generally bury `TAB()` inside a `PRINT` or an `LPRINT`. Here is where an example will help a lot. Suppose you wanted to print the word `Tampa` in column 20 and the word `Florida` in column 32. Why you would want to do that is beyond me! Anyway, this statement does the printing:

```
PRINT TAB(20); "Tampa"; TAB(32); "Florida"
```

Moving the Cursor Around the Screen

The `LOCATE` command moves the cursor to whatever row and column you want it to appear in. Suppose you want to print a title on the second line of the screen starting in the 20th column. You can use `LOCATE` to move the cursor, and then a `PRINT` will begin printing there. Here is the format of `LOCATE`:

```
LOCATE [row#] [, column#]
```

The *row#* must be a number from 1 to 25 (because there are 25 screen rows), and the *column#* must be from 1 to 80 (because, you guessed it, there are 80 columns). If you specify only the *row#* or the *column#*, then only that position is changed from the cursor's current placement. Here is the pair of statements that prints a message on row 5, column 36:

```
LOCATE 5, 36
PRINT "Get located!"
```

PSST! Use LOCATE to move the cursor all around the screen. You can even print "up" the screen by locating the cursor on a lower row and printing, then locating and printing on each row above the preceding one.

HMM... LOCATE enables you to overwrite parts of the screen you have already written to.

Beep-Beep!

Although you might not consider a bell ringing to be output, it is. When you want to get the user's attention, you can signal the user by buzzing the computer's bell with the BEEP command. Here is the format of BEEP:

BEEP

HMM... What could be easier? Every time QBasic comes across BEEP in your program, the computer's bell rings.

PSST! Adding a BEEP and blinking a message flashing in red letters will *really* get your user's attention if you need to!

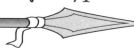

Print Formatting

There are two commands that correspond to `PRINT` and `LPRINT` called `PRINT USING` and `LPRINT USING`. There is a lot to the `USING` keyword, but most of the time you will need `USING` just to format numbers so that they print with a certain number of decimal places. Before looking at an example, take a look at the format of the `PRINT USING` command:

```
PRINT USING "formatString"; data
```

PSST!   The `LPRINT USING` command format looks just like that of `PRINT USING`.

The `formatString` is a string that contains the *look* that the `data` is to take. Often, you will see a *control code* inside the `formatString`. The control code is usually one of the following: #, ., ,, or &. When numbers are being printed, the # indicates a new digit in the number. For example, to print the number `456.7223` to one decimal place, you can use this:

```
PRINT USING "###.#"; 456.7223    ' Prints 456.7
```

YIKES!

Of course, if you wanted the number printed to one decimal place, you could have just printed `456.7`. The power of formatting shows itself when you print variables that contain data which needs formatting.

PSST!   The format strings round for you. Here is what you get if you print 456.7923 with the preceding format string:

456.8

If the number is smaller than the format string, QBasic pads with blanks. For example, the PRINT USING statement

```
PRINT USING "#####.## #####.## #####.##"; 5, 6, 7
```

prints this:

```
     5.00      6.00      7.00
```

If the number is larger than the format string you specify, QBasic prints the entire number with a percent sign, %, before it to get your attention that something is incorrect with the format string.

To print strings combined with numbers, you can use the & inside a format string to indicate the placement of the string. Study the following example PRINT USING statements to see how QBasic treats different versions of format strings.

```
' Short example to demonstrate USING format strings
num1 = 12345.67
st1$ = "Frank makes"
st2$ = "dollars a year"
PRINT USING "#####.#"; num1
PRINT USING "& #####.## &"; st1$; num1; st2$
PRINT USING "Frank makes $#####,.## dollars a year"; num1
END
```

Here is the output from these PRINT USING statements:

```
12345.7
Frank makes 12345.67 dollars a year
Frank makes $12,345.67 dollars a year
```

HMM...

Figure 8.1 helps explain the second PRINT USING statement. Remember that the format string simply describes how the subsequent data will look.

Figure 8.1.

The format string describes the look of the data being printed.

```
PRINT USING "& #####.## &"; st1$; num1; st2$
```

PSST!

Notice that if you precede the decimal point inside a format string with a comma, QBasic inserts commas where needed in the number.

YIKES!

PRINT USING is not exactly the easiest thing in the world to get familiar with. As mentioned earlier, you will most often use the ####.## code (with more or fewer pound signs depending on your needs) to print dollars and cents. Non-money values and strings typically print well without a USING format string.

Happy Hunting

 Relax! This chapter contained more details than any other so far. The rest of this book will use the material you learned here, so you'll get lots of review as you go along.

 Use COLOR to make your output screens more appealing.

 Use BEEP to get your user's attention.

 If you want to print dollar amounts, the PRINT USING command will help you format your output.

Charged

 Don't overdo COLOR and BEEP. Too much will confuse rather than help the user.

In Review

The goal of this chapter is to show you ways to liven your output by ringing the computer's bell and displaying colors on-screen. Of course, you can display colors only if your PC's hardware supports colors. Most people who own PCs have color monitors and adapter cards that can produce colorful output.

BEEP is one of the easiest commands in QBasic because it requires nothing but the single-word command BEEP to ring the computer's bell. The COLOR statement uses a table of color codes to set up the screen for colorful output. COLOR affects only future output, not printed output that is already on-screen when the COLOR command executes.

Code Example

```
BEEP
COLOR 4, 10    ' Green on red, Blecch!
PRINT "Hey, you're in the green!"
PRINT "You've sold QBasic programs and made a fortune!"
END
```

Code Analysis

This short program first rings the PC's bell and then changes the colors of screen output to green letters on a red background. The printed messages then appear in those colors.

Part III
QBasic and Math

"Hello, operator? Could you come over and help
me count ostrich eggs?"

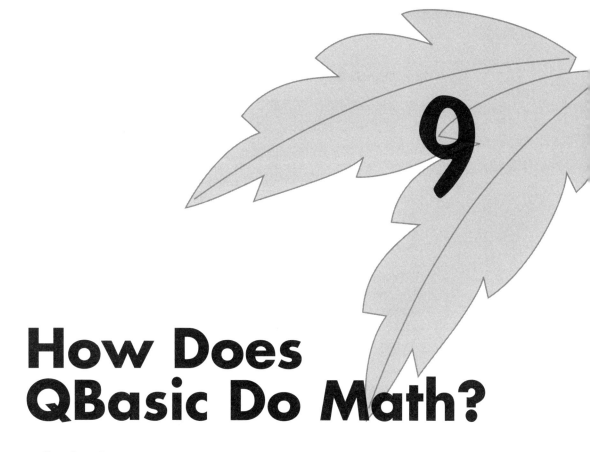

How Does QBasic Do Math?

With Operators

QBasic uses *operators* to perform math calculations. In Chapter 6, "How Do I Store Stuff?" you learned about four operators (the ones that add, subtract, multiply, and divide). There are more operators, and this chapter explains the additional ones. Not only must you understand the operators, but you must understand the *ordering* that QBasic uses to perform calculations using those operators.

QBasic does not always use a symbol, such as +, for its operators. The operator named MOD looks like a command. There is a good reason why QBasic, unlike most programming languages, does not stick to symbols for all of its operators. I just don't know what the reason is. Anyway, that's the way it is, and knowing that, you'll have fewer questions as you read through this chapter.

YIKES!

Don't you just hate math? If you do, you're in the right field because QBasic does your math for you if you learn how to set up the computations correctly.

Additional Operators

Table 9.1 lists the QBasic operators that are available in addition to +, -, *, and /. The sections that follow explain each of these additional operators.

Table 9.1. The additional QBasic operators.

Operator	Usage	Name and Description
^	2 ^ 5	Called the *exponentiation operator*, ^ raises a number to a specified power.

Operator	Usage	Name and Description
\	16 \ 3	Called the *integer division operator*, \ produces an integer result.
MOD	14 MOD 3	Called the *modulus operator*, MOD calculates the remainder after integer division takes place.

YIKES!

Don't confuse the integer division, \, with the regular division, /. They slant in opposite directions.

Exponentiation

The term *exponentiation* sounds a lot hairier than it really is. Even *math-sensitive* persons (the politically correct term these days for people who are math lame-brains) can understand raising numbers to powers. Often you see exponentiation written using a superscript for the exponent. In other words, if you were to see a 5 raised to the third power, you would see it written like this:

5^3

That means multiply 5 by itself three times: 5 times 5 times 5 is 125. In QBasic, we could store the same value in a variable by doing this:

```
ans = 5 ^ 3
```

Quickly, what is stored in ans in the next statement?

```
ans = 2 ^ 4
```

Because 2 ^ 4 means to multiply 2 times itself four times, and 2 times 2 times 2 times 2 equals 16, ans stores the number 16.

Skip This, It's Technical

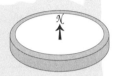

You can take the *n*th root of a number by raising it to a fractional value. For instance, to take the fifth root of 243, you could do this:

```
num = 243 ^ (1/5)
```

You'll read a little later in this chapter why the parentheses are needed. By the way, the fifth root of 243 is 3.

Integer Division with \

An integer is any number without a decimal point. Often we say that integers are whole numbers. All of these numbers are integers:

```
32      912     0      -121
```

None of these are integers:

```
32.333     0.0     -123.64     912.0
```

In a nutshell, using the \ tells QBasic to divide and throw away the remainder. Although 9 / 2 is 4.5, 9 \ 2 (notice that the *integer divide* sign was used) produces 4, which is the whole number answer.

Sometimes we can think of remainders as being whole numbers themselves. For instance, another way of looking at 9 / 2 is that it is 4 with a remainder of 1. The \ always produces the whole number portion. The next operator, MOD, returns the remainder.

PSST! Here's a neat use for the \ operator. Suppose you were writing a program that calculated change. To find out how many five-dollar bills were in the variable change, you could do this:

```
numFives = change \ 5
```

The MOD Squad

As just mentioned, MOD performs the other half of \. Whereas \ produces the integer portion of a division answer, MOD produces the integer remainder. Therefore, 9 MOD 2 produces an answer of 1 because 9 divided by 2 is 4 with a remainder of 1.

The following code reviews all the math operators:

```
PRINT "2 + 3 is"; 2 + 3
PRINT "6 - 4 is"; 6 - 4
PRINT "2 * 3 is"; 2 * 3
PRINT "12 / 7 is"; 12 / 7
PRINT "12 \ 7 is"; 12 \ 7
PRINT "12 MOD 7 is"; 12 MOD 7
PRINT "3 ^ 6 is"; 3 ^ 6
END
```

Here is the output from these PRINT statements:

```
2 + 3 is 5
6 - 4 is 2
2 * 3 is 6
12 / 7 is 1.714286
12 \ 7 is 1
12 MOD 7 is 5
3 ^ 6 is 729
```

Notice that you can print the results of calculations directly without having to store them in variables first.

PSST! Here's a good use for the immediate execution window at the bottom of the QBasic editing screen. Press F6 (the shortcut key to move between windows) and type PRINT 20 * 30. When you press Enter, QBasic displays the answer. Press any key and you're back to the editing window. You can try statements in the immediate execution window without affecting anything in the program itself.

The Order of Operators

QBasic does not always calculate from left to right. There is an order to QBasic's calculations. You'll find a table on the tear-out card called the Order of Operators table. This table explains that addition and subtraction are always calculated last no matter where they appear within other operators. For example, the following statement does *not* store 14 in ans:

```
ans = 3 + 4 * 2
```

A 14 would be stored in ans if QBasic did the addition first, but it does not. As the Order of Operators table tells you, multiplication is higher in the table, and therefore multiplication is said to *take precedence* over addition. Because the multiplication is performed first, the 4 is multiplied by the 2 to get 8, and *then* the 3 is added to the 8 to result in an 11 being stored in ans.

The parentheses take precedence over the other operators. Therefore, if you wanted the addition calculated first, you could group the addition inside parentheses like this:

```
ans = (3 + 4) * 2    ' A 14 is stored in ans now
```

Here is a long calculation with each step shown for you. If you
follow the Order of Operators, you'll understand how each step was
chosen.

```
ans = 6 + 40 - 8 / 2 MOD 3 * 2 ^ 3
                              \ /
      6 + 40 - 8 / 2 MOD 3 *  8
                  \ /
        6 + 40 - 4 MOD 3 * 8
                        \ /
          6 + 40 - 4 MOD 24
                    \  /
            6 + 40 - 4
            \ /
              46 - 4
              \ /
                42    (The value stored in ans)
```

Happy Hunting

 Let QBasic calculate everything for you.

 Use ^, MOD, and \ to compute exponentiation, remainder, and
integer division.

 Pay attention to the Order of Operators when setting up your
calculations.

 Use parentheses. Parentheses override the rest of the operator order, and they clearly express what you want done.

Charged

 Don't confuse the regular division operator, /, with the
integer division operator, \.

In Review

The goal of this chapter is to explore the QBasic operators and show you how they work. QBasic multiplies, adds, and subtracts in the way you would expect. There are three operators related to division: /, \, and MOD. The forward slash, /, divides two numbers as usual. The backslash, \, performs integer division. Integer division always produces a whole-number result and discards any remainder. The MOD operator picks up where \ leaves off by computing the remainder of an integer division. There is another operator, ^, which calculates exponentiation.

When you combine math operators, you must always be aware of QBasic's order of operation. QBasic always performs exponentiation before multiplication and division. QBasic saves addition and subtraction for last. You can override the order by adding parentheses to force evaluation of specific operations before the evaluation would normally take place.

Code Example

```
id = 100 \ 3     ' Integer division
PRINT "100 \ 3 is"; id
PRINT 1 + 2 + 3 + 4 + 5 * 2
PRINT (1 + 2 + 3 + 4 + 5) * 2
END
```

Code Analysis

The first two statements compute and print the integer division (no fraction or remainder is kept) of 100 divided by 3 (producing a value of 33). The next two PRINT statements produce very different values indeed. The first PRINT prints the value of 20 because the 5 * 2 results in 10 and the 1 and 2 and 3 and 4 are then added to the 10. In the second PRINT, the numbers 1 through 5 are first added, and the result, 15, is multiplied by 2 giving an answer of 30.

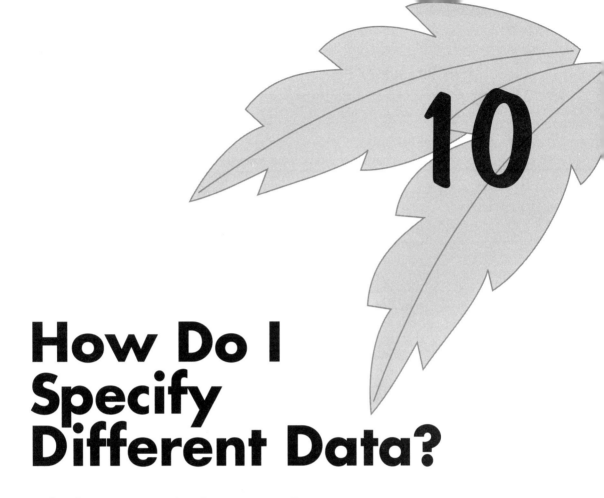

10

How Do I Specify Different Data?

With Extended Data Types

This chapter could be your least favorite in the book. It is not difficult or boring, but you might wonder why you need to know the material presented here. This chapter discusses the various *data types* in QBasic. You already know about two of them, numbers and strings. This chapter explains why there are different types of numbers and describes the various ways to specify each of the numeric data types.

As you read through the rest of the book, you'll better understand why these concepts are being taught here. When you want to work with a number that is extremely large, you might consider storing that number in a special kind of numeric variable designed to hold large numbers.

By the time you finish this chapter, you'll understand all the different variable suffix characters that QBasic offers as well. You already know that string variable names must end in dollar signs. The different numeric variables end in different data type suffix characters as well.

YIKES!

Stay with this chapter and your knowledge of it will pay dividends later. Some beginning QBasic programmers put off learning this chapter's material too long because it looks like a lot of math that they'll never need. Trust me, you'll need it again and again. QBasic does all the math for you as long as you understand how to set things up.

PSST!   Most of this chapter teaches you new terms that you'll need to understand as you progress through the rest of the book.

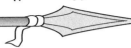

Literals and Constants

When you type a number or string in a QBasic program, you are typing a *constant* or a *literal*. Both words mean the same thing. Each of these are literals and constants:

```
534
-39.7
"Sally"
"1013 N. Illinois Ave."
```

The opposite of literals and constants are variables. The contents of variables can change (they *vary*, and that's why they're called *variables*).

Numeric Data Types

You already know what an integer is. The preceding chapter explained that an integer is a whole number without a decimal point. There are actually two kinds of QBasic integers: an integer and a *long integer*. The difference between them is determined by the range of numbers each can contain. Basically, a long integer can be larger than an integer. In a moment, you'll see the range of values that can appear in both kinds of integers.

The opposite of an integer is a *real number* (a number with a decimal point). However, as with integers, QBasic enables you to use two different kinds of real numbers depending on the range of values you want to represent. A *single-precision* number is one of QBasic's real number data types, and a *double-precision* number is the other kind of real number data type.

YIKES!

A table will help explain everything. Table 10.1 lists each of QBasic's numeric data types and the range of values that each can hold.

Table 10.1. **QBasic's numeric data types and their ranges.**

Data Type	Data Type Suffix	Range
Integer	%	-32768 to 32767
Long integer	&	-2147483648 to 2147483647
Single-precision	! (or none)	-3.402823×10^{38} to 3.402823×10^{38}
Double-precision	#	$-1.79769313486231 \times 10^{308}$ to $1.79769313486231 \times 10^{308}$

YIKES!

The funny-looking numbers in the last two entries of Table 10.1 are called *scientific notation*. You'll see how to interpret scientific notation numbers a little later in this chapter.

The primary reason for learning the different kinds of numbers is that there is a different kind of variable for each of those data types.

All the numeric variables you have used so far have been single-precision variables. But what if you wanted to store a huge number (such as a QBasic programmer's annual salary) in a variable? If you want to, you might have to use a larger precision variable.

Just as you use the dollar sign on string variables, you can use the data type suffixes in Table 10.1 to indicate a specific type of numeric variable. Here are some lines that store different values in each type of variable:

```
a% = 123              ' Integer
b& = 642346654        ' Long integer
c! = 532.34           ' Single-precision
d# = 39493344.233929  ' Double-precision
```

After you use a variable with a suffix, you must always use the suffix. In other words, don't name a variable `sales#` in the top of a program and then `sales` at the bottom. QBasic would think they were two different variables.

If you do not specify a data type suffix, QBasic assumes that the variable is single-precision. Therefore, these variables are identical and indicate the only data type suffix that is optional:

`myVal`

and

`myVal!`

YIKES!

If double-precision variables and long integer variables hold large numbers as well as small, why not always use them? It takes longer for QBasic to calculate and print the larger variables. Therefore, for efficiency, don't use the larger-precision variable types unless you really need to hold numbers within their wide ranges.

There is one last point you should understand: QBasic sometimes puts data type suffixes at the end of numeric constants, and you can do the same. QBasic does this to remind you that the number might be too large to fit within the smaller precision. For example, type the following line in QBasic:

```
i = 123456.78
```

What happened? QBasic immediately changed the statement to this:

```
i = 123456.78#
```

The variable i is single-precision because there is no # suffix and the value is small enough to fit in a single-precision variable. However, QBasic still insists on treating the number as if it were double-precision.

Scientific Notation

Don't let the name throw you! Scientific notation is easy to understand. Even if you don't ever plan to use scientific notation, QBasic sometimes displays results in scientific notation, so you should understand how to interpret it. (You also need to know what the last two lines in Table 10.1 mean!)

Scientific notation is a shortcut method for specifying extremely large or extremely small numbers. All QBasic scientific notation values have a D or an E in them. The D represents a double-precision number; the E, single-precision.

YIKES!

Why they didn't use S for single-precision is one of the world's greatest mysteries.

Here are some values in scientific notation:

```
3.65E+4      -756.423D+265      -9.1E-2      -122325.6433D-101
```

To find out exactly what value is represented by a number in scientific notation, take the number to the left of the E or D and multiply it by 10 raised to the number on the right of the E or D. In other words, 3.65E+4 is exactly the same as 3.65 times 10^4, or 36500.

PSST!
All you have to do is move the decimal point to the left or right the number of places indicated by the rightmost digit. If the rightmost digit (the number following the D or E) has a plus sign, move the decimal to the right, and if the number has a minus sign, move the decimal to the left.

HMM...   Table 10.1 shows that a double-precision variable can hold a number as large as 1.79769313486231 multiplied by 10 followed by 308 zeros!

Happy Hunting

 Get comfortable with the fact that numbers and strings are called both constants and literals. They do not change (but variables can change).

 Use a long integer or double-precision variable suffix if you are storing extremely small or extremely large numbers.

Charged

 Don't store values in long integer or double-precision variables unless you need the extreme ranges they offer.

In Review

The goal of this chapter is to show you how to determine exactly what kind of numeric variables you are working with. The information presented here is not always considered to be the most exciting in QBasic, but you will be grateful that you now understand it when QBasic spits out a number with a trailing pound sign (#); you now know that the pound sign is just an indicator of the value's data type, namely double-precision.

Reserve the use of long integer and double-precision variables for variables that need to hold extremely large or extremely small data values. For everyday values used in most games, in business, and even in scientific programs, the integer and single-precision variables work best because they are more efficient than the longer variable data types.

Code Example

```
n% = 55                ' Integer
weight! = 165.75       ' Single-precision
salary = 1987.23       ' Single-precision
atomicWeight# = -0.0000022233333#   ' Double-precision
```

Code Analysis

These lines of code assign values to the different numeric data types. The first variable, n%, is an integer and holds the integer 55. The second variable, weight!, is single-precision and holds 165.75. The third variable, salary, is also single-precision. (Numeric variables without an exclamation point after their names are automatically single-precision.) The last variable, atomicWeight#, holds an extremely small number and is a double-precision variable.

What Math Can QBasic Do?

Use Numeric Functions to Find Out

Are you thinking, "Oh no, not more math!"? Well, fear not, because this chapter makes QBasic do all the work. QBasic is a programming language that can perform simple calculations and complex calculations—all you have to do is type the correct name for the routine you want performed. This chapter is the last of the math-oriented chapters in the book. Programming computers is not for math experts—programming computers is for anybody.

QBasic supplies many built-in *functions*. A function is the term given to routines inside the QBasic language that calculate and manipulate data. The only reason that functions are not called commands is because of their nature. Commands control a program's execution, whereas functions convert values into other values.

HMM...   Some of the functions described here do require trigonometric or scientific skills to understand, but you can safely skip those. Only the programmers who need them have to understand them.

All QBasic functions have names, and most of them end with parentheses. You have already seen one function in this book: TAB(). TAB() takes the value inside its parentheses (called the *argument*) and sends the cursor to that column position on the screen.

The Integer Functions

There are several built-in functions that return the integer portion of their arguments. In other words, if you put a double-precision value inside these functions' parentheses, they compute the integer portion of the number. The easiest function to learn is INT(), which returns the integer portion of a number. The following statement stores a 12 in ans:

```
ans = INT(12.4445533)    ' Stores a 12 in ans
```

You can also print the value of a function. This next statement prints a 12 on-screen:

```
PRINT INT(12.4445533)      ' Prints a 12
```

 PSST! A function is like a box in that you put something into the top of it and something else comes out the bottom. Figure 11.1 shows you what the INT() function's box would look like.

Figure 11.1.

INT( ) is like a magic box that accepts an argument and returns an integer value based on that argument.

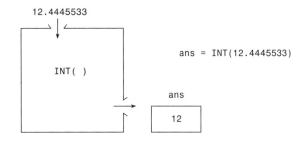

A function's argument can be a constant or a variable.

HMM...

INT() does not round. INT() was written to return the closest integer *smaller* than the argument. This means that if you pass INT() a negative number, INT() returns the *next smallest* integer, which will be the next lowest negative number. The following example prints a -6 because -6 is the closest integer that is smaller than -5.4:

```
PRINT INT(-5.4)      ' Prints -6
```

QBasic supplies two other similar functions, FIX() and CINT(). These functions both convert their arguments to integers differently than INT(). FIX() *truncates* its fractional portion. *Truncate* is a fancy word meaning that whatever is to the right of the whole value is chopped off; for example, -5.4 becomes -5 and 6.4 becomes 6.

CINT() (for *convert integer*) does round the way you would expect. CINT() rounds the value to the nearest integer. Therefore, the following example prints -6, 5, and 6:

```
PRINT CINT(-5.8)        ' Prints -6
PRINT CINT(5.4)         ' Prints 5
PRINT CINT(5.5001)      ' Prints 6
```

Because the argument you want converted might be a large value whose integer portion requires a long integer result, QBasic supplies yet another function, called CLNG() (for *convert long*). This function converts its argument to a long integer. The following example stores 12345678 (an integer too large to fit in a regular integer variable) in longNum&:

```
longNum& = CLNG(12345678.345432784#)
```

Timing Yourself

QBasic supplies an interesting function that is one of the few functions which do not take parentheses because you do not pass an argument. The TIMER function returns the number of seconds since your computer's internal clock struck midnight.

You might wonder why you would ever need to know how many seconds have elapsed since midnight. Suppose you were timing an event. You might want to ask the user a question and decide how long it took the user to answer. You can save the value of TIMER before you ask the user, then subtract that value from the value of TIMER *after* the user answers. The difference is the number of seconds the user took to answer. Here is a program that does just that:

```
' Program that times the user's response
CLS
before = TIMER      ' Save the time before asking
INPUT "What is 20 + 35"; ans
after = TIMER       ' Save the time after answering
diff = after - before
PRINT "It took you only"; diff; "seconds to answer!"
END
```

Randomizing

There is a way to make computers generate different answers with the very same program! You might wonder why you would ever need to do that, but think about game programs for a moment. If the slot machine in the back of the book always produced the same set of slot pulls every time you played the game, the game would be boring, wouldn't it? QBasic contains the RND() function to return a random number.

Before using RND(), you should use the RANDOMIZE statement. RANDOMIZE *seeds the random-number generator*. This means that a value you supply with the RANDOMIZE command acts as a trigger for a new set of random values. If you supply a different RANDOMIZE value every time you run a program, the program's RND() function returns a different set of values each time.

Here is the format of RANDOMIZE:

RANDOMIZE *seedValue*

Most of the time, QBasic programmers use the TIMER function in place of a *seedValue* like this:

RANDOMIZE TIMER

Because your computer's internal clock is different every time you run a program, you will produce truly random numbers after seeding the random-number generator with TIMER. This is the method used by the slot machine program in Appendix B. After you RANDOMIZE the random-number generator, the RND() function will produce random results.

RND() always returns a random number from 0 to 1. Here is some code that prints three random numbers on-screen each time you run it:

```
RANDOMIZE TIMER      ' Seed the internal random generator
PRINT RND
PRINT RND
PRINT RND
END
```

If you want something else, such as a number from 1 to 6 as you would get when simulating a dice roll, you can perform a little calculation like this:

```
PRINT INT(RND * 6) + 1
                    ' Ensure the random number is from 1 to 6
```

Some Really Hard Functions

Fun Fact
Mathematicians have tons of formulas they can apply to a computer's random-number sequence to see how statistically random they (the numbers, not the mathematicians!) are.

This section briefly explains the trigonometric and scientific functions that QBasic supplies. Glance through them and remember they are here. If you ever need these functions, you can come back here for guidance, but if you don't think you will, you are safe to skip them.

Table 11.1 lists the remaining built-in math functions discussed in this book. After you are through, you can take a break. The next chapter describes many of QBasic's string functions, which are fun even for nontechnical people.

Table 11.1. Some of QBasic's other math functions.

Function	Description
ABS()	Returns the positive equivalent (absolute value) of whatever value you pass it.
ATN()	Computes the arc tangent of the argument in radians.
COS()	Computes the cosine of the argument in radians.
EXP()	Computes the base of the natural logarithm (also known by mathematicians as *e*) raised to the power specified by the argument.
LOG()	Computes the natural logarithm of the function's argument.
SIN()	Computes the sine of the argument in radians.
SQR()	Computes the square root of its argument.
TAN()	Computes the tangent of the argument in radians.

Skip This, It's Technical

If you want to specify a trig function's argument in degrees rather than in radians, you can do so. Multiply the degree value by 3.141592654 (the approximate value of *pi*), and then divide that by 180. If you want to get the arc tangent of 90 degrees, the following statement does just that:

```
ac90 = ATN(90 * 3.141592654 / 180)
```

Happy Hunting

 Use the built-in math functions instead of writing your own code to do the same thing.

 Use TIMER when you want to time any event within your program, such as the user's response time to a question.

Charged

 Don't confuse INT(), CINT(), CLNG(), and FIX(). These functions seem to do the same things, but they sometimes return slightly different integer values.

 To produce truly random values, place a RANDOMIZE TIMER statement at the top of any program that uses RND(). The program then produces a different set of random numbers each time you run it.

 Don't feel as if you have to master all the math functions at once. If you don't need the trig functions, you can safely skip them.

In Review

The goal of this chapter is to show you how to streamline your routines by using some of QBasic's built-in math functions. There are integer functions that round numbers to integers in different ways, a random function that returns a random number, and a timer function (appropriately named TIMER) that returns a value based on your PC's internal clock.

Depending on your needs, you might want to use some of the more complicated scientific and trigonometric functions too.

Code Example

```
PRINT "The number of seconds since midnight is"; TIMER
PRINT "You likely know that 6.7777 rounded up is"; CINT(6.777)
PRINT "How old are you"; age
RANDOMIZE age
        ' Seed the random-number generator on the user's age
PRINT "Here's a random number:"; RND
PRINT "The number of seconds since midnight now is"; TIMER
```

Code Analysis

The program first prints the number of seconds since midnight using the TIMER function. TIMER is nice to use (as is done here) to show the beginning and ending times of a program to see how long the program takes to run. Also, you can divide the value returned by TIMER to arrive at hours and minutes if you need to.

The CINT() function rounds values the way you would expect: The numbers round up or down to the nearest integer.

Before using a random number from RND, you might first want to seed the random-number generator with a value (the TIMER value is usually different enough to use) so that a different RND value is generated every time you call the RND function. This program uses the user's age to seed the random-number generator before printing a random number. If the same age is entered every time this program is run, the same random number will appear.

12

Can QBasic Do Much with Strings?

Check Out QBasic's Built-In String Functions

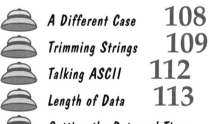

QBasic is known as one of the best programming languages for string manipulation. Although QBasic is often touted as a *beginner's language* (it is, but it's good for pros too), QBasic excels over C, Pascal, FORTRAN, and the other languages when it comes to working with strings. The primary reason that QBasic is so string-strong is because of the built-in string-manipulation functions described in this chapter.

Most of QBasic's string functions take a string as their argument and return a string based on that argument. Most of QBasic's string function names end with a dollar sign indicating that they return strings.

A Different Case

QBasic includes two built-in string functions that convert from uppercase to lowercase and vice versa. A short example will demonstrate their usage. The following lines contain code that assigns two strings, each containing both uppercase and lowercase letters, to variables. Both variables are passed through the UCASE$() and LCASE$() functions. UCASE$() converts its string argument to all uppercase letters, and LCASE$() converts its string argument to lowercase letters.

```
first$ = "Example #1 of a STRing."
second$ = "Example #2 of a STRing."
newFirst$ = UCASE$(first$)
newSecond$ = LCASE$(second$)
PRINT newFirst$
PRINT newSecond$
```

Here is the output from the code:

```
EXAMPLE #1 OF A STRING.
example #2 of a string.
```

Notice that both UCASE$() and LCASE$() ignore any characters that are not alphabetic.

PSST!

UCASE$() leaves uppercase letters unchanged, and LCASE$() leaves lowercase letters unchanged.

Trimming Strings

QBasic continues the long-standing BASIC tradition of providing three functions that return the left, right, and middle portions of strings. These three function names are LEFT$(), RIGHT$(), and MID$(). The LEFT$() and RIGHT$() functions are the easiest to use because they take fewer arguments than MID$().

LEFT$() returns the left portion of a string, and RIGHT$() returns the right portion of a string. For example, assume that you assign the letters ABCDEFG to a string like this:

```
letter$ = "ABCDEFG"
```

You can print various portions of the left part of the string with LEFT$(). The remarks to the right of the following PRINT statements describe what gets printed.

```
PRINT LEFT$(letter$, 1)       ' Prints A
PRINT LEFT$(letter$, 2)       ' Prints AB
PRINT LEFT$(letter$, 3)       ' Prints ABC
PRINT LEFT$(letter$, 6)       ' Prints ABCDEF
PRINT LEFT$(letter$, 22)      ' Prints ABCDEFG
```

The second argument of LEFT$() indicates how much of the left part of the string you want the function to return. If you like, you can assign the left part of a string to another string variable like this:

```
firstName$ = LEFT$(fullName$, 5)
```

YIKES!

If the second argument of LEFT$() is longer than the string itself (as in the last of the preceding five PRINT statements), QBasic does not display an error but simply returns the entire string.

RIGHT$() is easy because it works just like LEFT$() except that it returns the rightmost portion of strings. The following PRINT statement prints FL:

```
city$ = "Miami, FL"
PRINT RIGHT$(city$, 2)       ' Prints FL
```

The MID$() function returns the middle of a string. You must give MID$() three arguments because MID$() must know where to begin pulling out characters from a string and how many to pull. Here is the format of MID$():

```
MID$(string, start [, length])
```

HMM...

If you do not specify a *length*, QBasic returns the entire string to the right of the *start* position.

Here is a program that shows you how to print *substrings* (portions of a string) from a longer string:

```
' Illustrates the MID$() function
CLS
words$ = "Rome Venice Florence Verona Milan"
PRINT "Italian cities to visit:"
PRINT MID$(words$, 1, 4)      ' Prints Rome
PRINT MID$(words$, 6, 6)      ' Prints Venice
PRINT MID$(words$, 13, 8)     ' Prints Florence
PRINT MID$(words$, 22, 6)     ' Prints Verona
PRINT MID$(words$, 29, 5)     ' Prints Milan
END
```

HMM... You can see a good use of a couple of these string functions in Appendix B's slot machine game. Early in the game, the player has the option of continuing (by pressing Enter) or stopping by typing STOP. The program converts the user's input to uppercase and then checks the leftmost character in the string by combining UCASE$() and LEFT$() with this line:

```
IF (UCASE$(LEFT$(ent$, 1)) = "S") THEN
```

You'll learn about IF in the next chapter. The combined use of UCASE$() and LEFT$() is the important point right now.

PSST! Figure 12.1 makes the three substring functions even clearer by showing you how they would work on a single string.

Figure 12.1.

Using the LEFT$(), MID$(), and RIGHT$() string functions.

LEFT$ (m$, 8)   RIGHT$ (m$, 9)

m$ = "The rain in Spain needs to drain."

MID$ (m$, 13, 5)

Talking ASCII

You will find an *ASCII table* in Appendix C. ASCII (pronounced *ask-ee*—so if you want to *know-ee* you can just hop to Appendix C and *ask-ee*) is a code that maps a different number to each character that your computer can produce. (The first 31 ASCII codes represent *nonprintable characters,* which are codes that control computer operations such as form feeding a new page on your printer.)

Not all the ASCII table's characters appear on your keyboard. You might need to produce one of the characters that is not on your keyboard. For instance, you might want to print the symbol listed at position 172 in the ASCII table (a one-fourth symbol). To do so, use the CHR$() function. Put the ASCII code inside the parentheses, and QBasic returns that ASCII's symbol. The following line prints the one-fourth symbol:

```
PRINT CHR$(172)
```

The ASC() function does just the opposite. ASC() takes a string argument and returns the ASCII code for the first character in that string. The following line assigns the number 67 to the variable named ascCode because 67 is the ASCII value for the letter *C*:

```
ascCode = ASC("C")
```

PSST!   You will use CHR$() much more often than ASC() because you will often need to print and work with characters that aren't on your keyboard.

Length of Data

The LEN() function works with both numbers and strings. LEN() returns the number of characters of memory needed to store its argument. For instance, the string QBasic takes six memory locations because there are six characters in QBasic. Therefore, n is assigned a 6 in this statement:

```
n = LEN("QBasic")
```

To find out how much memory a number takes, use the number in LEN() like this:

```
N# = 23.3#
PRINT "Double-precision numbers take"; LEN(N#); " locations."
```

Getting the Date and Time

Perhaps two of the easiest functions are DATE$ and TIME$. It doesn't take a nuclear chemist to figure out that these functions return the date and time, respectively. Unlike most of QBasic's string functions, DATE$ and TIME$ don't require arguments, so they do not use parentheses. The following statements print the date and assign the time to a variable:

```
PRINT "The date is "; DATE$ ' Might print The date is 12-18-95
t$ = TIME$                  ' Might assign 16:23:55 to t$
```

The time is returned in the 24-hour military clock time of your computer. Therefore, any hour past 12:00 noon will be greater than 12. The time assigned to t$ in the preceding code would be 4:23 in the afternoon (the seconds are 55).

HMM...

The time had to be assigned to a string variable because both DATE$ and TIME$ return the date and time as strings.

YIKES!

If your computer's internal clock is not set properly, DATE$ and TIME$ won't return correct values.

Happy Hunting

 Use the built-in string functions to access and manipulate string data.

 Convert from uppercase to lowercase and back again with UCASE$() and LCASE$().

 Return parts of a string with LEFT$(), RIGHT$(), and MID$().

 Use CHR$() and the ASCII table to produce characters from your programs that aren't on your keyboard.

Charged

 Don't expect a.m. or p.m. times with TIME$. TIME$ returns a 24-hour time.

In Review

The goal of this chapter is to extend your knowledge of built-in functions by showing you some of QBasic's string functions. The string functions are some of the richest in any programming language. Most languages play catch-up to QBasic when it comes to string manipulation.

You learned how to retrieve parts of a string and convert strings to uppercase and lowercase letters. The ASCII table also helps QBasic programmers print characters that don't even appear on the computer's keyboard.

The TIME$ and DATE$ functions enable you to get the computer's current time and date when needed. Often, programmers like to print the date and time at the top of a report to show exactly when the report was printed.

Code Example

```
INPUT "What is your name"; nam$
PRINT "Your first initial is "; LEFT$(nam$, 1)
PRINT "The last letter in your name is "; RIGHT$(nam$, 1)
PRINT "Your first letter's ASCII code is"; ASC(LEFT$(nam$, 1))
PRINT "In uppercase, your name looks like "; UCASE$(nam$)
PRINT "In lowercase, your name looks like "; LCASE$(nam$)
PRINT "Set your clock; the time is "; TIME$
```

Code Analysis

These lines of code use many of the functions taught in this chapter. The string used in most of the functions is the user's name. The PRINT statements before each function call describe exactly what is being done in the corresponding function calls. Notice that the fourth line in the program uses an embedded function call (called a *nested function call*). The user's first initial is picked off the nam$ string, and the ASCII code for that letter is then printed.

Part IV
QBasic Takes Control

"The secret to riding the vines is good loop control!"

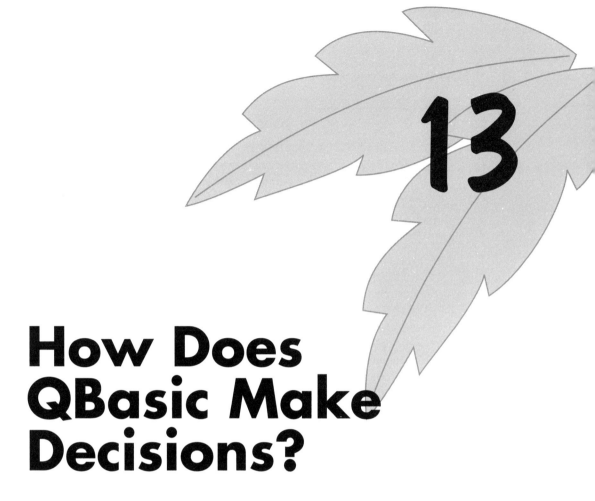

How Does QBasic Make Decisions?

With Relational Operators

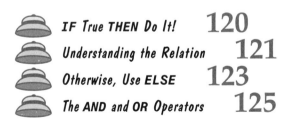

It is possible to write extremely smart QBasic programs. Of course, being smart doesn't mean that your computer can think on its own. Computers cannot think, but they can make decisions if you teach them how to do so. You must use decision-making operators and statements if you want QBasic to make decisions.

You would want QBasic to make decisions so that the programs you write will be more beneficial to you. QBasic can look at data inside variables and determine a course of action based on statements in the program. For example, if a certain sales level is not met, you might want your QBasic program to print an exception report. If the sales level is exceeded, you might want a completely different set of statements to execute, perhaps to print a congratulatory message or to add bonus pay to the sales staff's paychecks.

This chapter begins to show you how to instruct QBasic to execute one part or another part of your programs. Until now, QBasic executed each statement in the program, one line after another. Before you are through with this chapter, you'll know how to instruct QBasic to ignore a section of your program if the data warrants it.

IF True THEN Do It!

The IF statement is QBasic's decision statement. Most programming languages offer an IF statement, and QBasic is no exception. The IF statement is the first QBasic statement you've seen that spans more than one line of a program. Here is the format of IF:

```
IF relation THEN
    Block of one or more QBasic statements
END IF
```

PSST!   The multiple-line IF always ends with the END IF statement. The *Block* of statements that goes between IF and END IF might contain one or many statements.

The `Block` of statements might or might not execute, depending on the `relation`. Before studying what the `relation` means, consider this idea: The designers of QBasic didn't set out to design QBasic to be hard to use. They designed QBasic to be easy. The `IF` works just as it does in spoken language. For instance, think about how this spoken statement works:

"If the password is correct, you can go into the room."

The spoken *if* determines whether the remaining statement is allowed. The QBasic `IF` determines whether the `Block of one or more QBasic statements` executes.

Understanding the Relation

To understand the `relation`, you have to learn six more QBasic operators, known as the *relational operators.* (Sometimes the relational operators are known as the *conditional operators,* and sometimes the `relation` is known as a *condition.*) Table 13.1 lists the six relational operators and gives an example `IF` statement for each operator.

Table 13.1. **The relational operators.**

Operator	Description	Example
>	Greater than	`IF sales > 1200 THEN`
<	Less than	`IF salary < 400.50 THEN`
>=	Greater than or equal to	`IF (bonus >= expected) THEN`
<=	Less than or equal to	`IF age <= MinAge THEN`
=	Equal to	`IF (score = highScore) THEN`
<>	Not equal to	`IF answer$ <> "YES" THEN`

PSST!   Notice that the *relation* is often enclosed in parentheses, but the parentheses are not required.

Suppose your program needs to ask the user how many sales calls were made that day. If the user made more than 10 sales calls, you want the program to congratulate the effort. If 10 or fewer sales calls were made, you want the program to continue without doing anything extra. In other words, *if the number of sales calls was greater than 10, print a message.* That statement translates directly into the following code:

```
INPUT "How many sales calls did you make today"; numCalls
IF (numCalls > 10) THEN
    BEEP
    PRINT "Wow, good job!  You are working hard!"
END IF
' Rest of program would follow
```

The program beeps and congratulates the salesperson if the number of sales calls was more than 10.

HMM...   If the *relation* is false, the statement following IF does not execute. Therefore, if the number of sales calls was 10 or less, the user never knows about the congratulatory message. The IF has forced certain lines of code to execute only if a given condition is true.

It is fine to use strings on either side of the relational operators. QBasic uses Appendix C's ASCII table to determine whether one string is less than another (notice that uppercase letters come before lowercase, so Tucson would compare less than tuba). Here is a program that asks the user a question about a new baby:

```
INPUT "Is your baby a girl"; ans$
IF (ans$ = "yes") THEN
    PRINT "I bet she's cute!"
END IF
```

PSST! What if the answer is YES (in uppercase letters)? The IF would compare false, because to a computer, uppercase letters are different from lowercase (the ASCII table tells us so). You learned in the preceding chapter how to fix this potential problem. Use LCASE$() like this:

```
INPUT "Is your baby a girl"; ans$
IF (LCASE$(ans$) = "yes") THEN
    PRINT "I bet she's cute!"
END IF
```

Otherwise, Use ELSE

The IF statements you have seen have been called *single-leg* IF statements. In other words, you have decided what code will execute if the *relation* is true. What, however, if you want one of *two* sets of statements to execute depending on the data being tested? In the IF right before this section, nothing prints if the baby is a boy. You might want to print one message if the baby is a girl and another if the baby is a boy. Do you think the following code will accomplish that?

```
INPUT "Is your baby a girl"; ans$
IF (LCASE$(ans$) = "yes") THEN
    PRINT "I bet she's cute!"
END IF
PRINT "He'll be a handsome sports star some day!"
```

YIKES!

This IF does not fix anything! If the baby is a boy, the boy's message prints. However, if the baby is a girl, *both* the girl's and the boy's messages print! Remember that when the END IF is over, the rest of the program executes line-by-line as usual.

You can add the ELSE keyword to an IF statement whenever you want to specify two sets of code. The first set executes if the *relation* is true, and the other executes if the *relation* is false. Here is the complete format of IF with the ELSE keyword:

```
IF relation THEN
    Block of one or more QBasic statements
[ELSE
    Block of one or more QBasic statements]
END IF
```

PSST!  ELSE is optional, as the brackets in the format indicate. However, when you want to specify two sets of relational code, ELSE is needed.

Many teachers and books make too much out of the ELSE and confuse QBasic students when ELSE is actually straightforward. Consider this section of code:

```
INPUT "Is your baby a girl"; ans$
IF (LCASE$(ans$) = "yes") THEN
    PRINT "I bet she's cute!"
ELSE
    PRINT "He'll be a handsome sports star some day!"
END IF
```

HMM... The indention after IF and ELSE is not required because QBasic is a free-form language. However, indenting the lines of code that form the two legs of an IF-ELSE statement helps each set stand apart and makes debugging easier.

If the baby is a girl, the girl's message displays on-screen. If the baby is a boy, the boy's message displays. The IF-ELSE is an extremely

readable statement. Here is a written description (often called *pseudocode* or *false code*) of the IF statement you just saw:

```
Ask whether the user's baby is a girl.
If the baby is a girl, print "I bet she's cute!"
otherwise, print "He'll be a handsome sports star some day!"
Continue with the rest of the program.
```

The AND and OR Operators

Sometimes the relational operators are not quite enough to test for all the conditions you need to test for. You can combine two relational operators together with the AND and OR keywords. As with ELSE, AND and OR read a lot like their spoken counterparts. Consider this code:

```
IF (inventoryTotal > 35000) AND (numSalespeople < 4) THEN
   PRINT "Hire more salespeople!"
END IF
' Rest of program would go here
```

If the total dollar amount of the inventory (stored in inventoryTotal) is more than $35,000 and if the number of salespeople on the staff (stored in numSalespeople—see how descriptive variable names help you understand programs faster?) is less than four, the program prints a message. In other words, the message prints only if *both* of the *relation*s on either side of AND are true. If either is false, the message does not print.

If the OR keyword had been used rather than AND, a different IF would have taken place. The code

```
IF (inventoryTotal > 35000) OR (numSalespeople < 4) THEN
   PRINT "Hire more salespeople!"
END IF
' Rest of program would go here
```

prints the message if *either* the inventory total is less than $35,000 *or* the number of sales people is less than four. An OR condition is more likely to test true than an AND condition because only one side of OR has to be true for the entire IF's *relation* to be true.

YIKES!

Not all the snippets of code presented throughout these chapters comprise a complete program. It is assumed that statements would appear before and after the code presented. Only enough of the code is given at a time to zero in on the command or function being described.

PSST!  AND and OR are actually operators. They are called the *logical operators,* or the *compound relational operators.*

HMM... Appendix B's slot machine game uses several IF statements. Right before the program ends, you'll find the following IF statement, which prints a message depending on how much money the player loses:

```
IF (totalCash <= 0) THEN
    PRINT "Too bad. Hope you have a ticket home."
    PRINT "Come back when you've got more money."
ELSE
    PRINT "You are leaving with some money, which is more than"
    PRINT "I can say for a lot of people!  Thanks for playing!"
END IF
```

Happy Hunting

 Use IF to test a condition and execute certain lines of code according to the results of the test.

 Specify an ELSE section if you want one set of code or another set of code to execute depending on the result of the IF's *relation*.

 Feel free to test strings for equality in an IF's *relation* test. QBasic uses the ASCII table to determine the result of the test.

Charged

 Don't forget that the THEN keyword must follow the IF's *relation*.

 Don't forget to convert the user's input to uppercase (with UCASE$()) or lowercase (with LCASE$()) before comparing. You never know whether the user typed the input with the Caps Lock key on.

In Review

The goal of this chapter is to show you how the IF statement works. You can now tell your computer to make decisions about which lines in a program to execute. The IF statement uses the true or false result of relational operators to see whether one set of code should execute.

By adding the ELSE clause to the end of IF, you can cause one of two sets of QBasic statements to execute depending on the result of a relational test.

Code Example

```
INPUT "Are you a local or visitor (L or V)"; ans$
ans$ = UCASE$(ans$) ' Convert the user's response to uppercase
IF (ans$ = "L") THEN
   PRINT "You get in free because you pay state taxes!"
   PRINT "Go on in."
ELSE
   PRINT "Welcome to our state! We'd like to welcome you"
   PRINT "and charge you only a nominal fee for entrance."
END IF
```

Code Analysis

The program first asks the user to indicate a home-state location. The user enters either an L or a V according to the user's status. Just in case the user types a lowercase letter, the second line in the program converts the letter to uppercase before the IF takes off.

The IF statement then prints one of two messages depending on the user's response. This action is why IF helps QBasic make decisions: One or the other set of PRINT statements executes, but you have no idea which set will execute when you write the program. The set executed is up to QBasic when the program is run.

Will QBasic Work with Lots of Decisions?

Learn SELECT CASE and See

 A Case for **SELECT CASE** 130

This chapter presents one of the hardest-looking QBasic statements in the book, SELECT CASE. The neat thing about SELECT CASE, however, is that it is really one of the easiest to use! SELECT CASE takes up where IF leaves off. By combining relational tests and the AND and OR operators, you can use IF to compare several relationships of data as explained in the preceding chapter. However, if you need to compare more than two or three data relationships, the IF-ELSE statement is too cumbersome to use.

By using SELECT CASE, you can cause your QBasic program to select from one of many conditions and execute certain statements accordingly. The SELECT CASE statement has several formats, but they all basically take on the same general look. Here is the most common (and easiest) SELECT CASE statement:

```
SELECT CASE expression
CASE value
   Block of one or more QBasic statements
CASE value
   Block of one or more QBasic statements
[CASE value
   Block of one or more QBasic statements]
[CASE ELSE
   Block of one or more QBasic statements]
END SELECT
```

YIKES!

Yes, SELECT CASE might look difficult, but you'll see that it's a piece of cake.

A Case for SELECT CASE

In a nutshell, the SELECT CASE statement selects one set of statements, from several possible cases, that matches an expression. The SELECT CASE often replaces an IF within an IF within an IF (and so forth).

Perhaps the best use of SELECT CASE is programming a *menu* of
choices. A computer menu is often useful for helping a user decide
on a series of actions. You already have seen the QBasic menu
system. Instead of having to remember a bunch of commands for
saving a program or running a program, you only have to select
from a list across the top of the screen called a menu. You can add a
menu to your own programs so that your users can select from a
series of things they might want to do.

Suppose you were writing a program for your banker friend who
needed certain calculations done throughout the day. You might
write a program that contained the following menu:

```
Here are your banking calculation choices:
 1. Calculate current ratio
 2. Calculate net working capital
 3. Calculate average payment period
 4. Calculate average collection period
What is your choice?
```

YIKES!

Don't concern yourself with what these calculations are all
about. A banker understands them. The SELECT CASE, not
the calculations, is our primary consideration here.

The following program would take care of the banker's needs just
fine. Follow the program to see how SELECT CASE chooses among
possible actions. If the banker's menu selection (stored in choice) is
1, the first CASE executes, and the other CASEs take care of the other
possibilities:

```
CLS
' Program that performs banking analysis
PRINT "B a n k e r ' s    C a l c u l a t o r"
PRINT
PRINT "Here are your banking calculation choices:"
PRINT
PRINT " 1. Calculate current ratio"
```

```
PRINT " 2. Calculate net working capital"
PRINT " 3. Calculate average payment period"
PRINT " 4. Calculate average collection period"
PRINT
INPUT "What is your choice"; choice
PRINT
' Let the SELECT CASE decide the proper course of action
SELECT CASE choice
CASE 1:
   INPUT "What are the current assets"; ca
   INPUT "What are the current liabilities"; cl
   cr = ca / cl
   PRINT USING "& #.##"; "The current ratio is"; cr
CASE 2:
   INPUT "What are the current assets"; ca
   INPUT "What are the current liabilities"; cl
   nwc = ca - cl
   PRINT USING "& $#####,."; "The net working capital is"; nwc
CASE 3:
   INPUT "What are the accounts payable"; ap
   INPUT "What are the credit purchases"; cp
   app = (ap / cp) * 360
   PRINT USING "& ## &"; "The average payment period is";
                app; "days"
CASE 4:
   INPUT "What are the accounts receivable"; ar
   INPUT "What are the net credit sales"; ncs
   acp = (ar / ncs) * 360
   PRINT USING "& ## &"; "The average collection period is";
                acp; "days"
CASE ELSE:
   BEEP
   PRINT "** You did not enter a correct choice **"
END SELECT
END
```

HMM... As many statements as you want can appear after each CASE.

PSST!   The CASE ELSE handles the action that takes place if the user's input does not match any of the other CASEs. The CASE ELSE is optional but strongly recommended to take care of incorrect data.

To give you an idea of how this program flows, here are two runs of the program. Trace the program listing as you follow both of them:

```
B a n k e r ' s   C a l c u l a t o r

Here are your banking calculation choices:

  1. Calculate current ratio
  2. Calculate net working capital
  3. Calculate average payment period
  4. Calculate average collection period

What is your choice? 3

What are the accounts payable? 2689
What are the credit purchases? 31093
The average payment period is 31 days
```

PSST!   In the next run, the user did not enter a proper menu selection, so the CASE ELSE had to take over:

```
B a n k e r ' s   C a l c u l a t o r

Here are your banking calculation choices:

  1. Calculate current ratio
  2. Calculate net working capital
  3. Calculate average payment period
  4. Calculate average collection period

What is your choice? 6

** You did not enter a correct choice **
```

HMM...

In the next chapter, you'll learn how to repeat a series of statements so that the menu reappears after a calculation has been made. The user then will not have to rerun the program to request another calculation.

Happy Hunting

 Use SELECT CASE to execute a set of QBasic statements based on one of several possible choices.

 Always specify a CASE ELSE to handle bad data that might slip into a SELECT CASE expression variable.

 You can use either integers or character strings for the SELECT CASE test *expression* and CASEs.

Charged

 Don't be thrown by the strange-looking format of SELECT CASE. SELECT CASE simply chooses from one of several sets of code based on a matching CASE expression.

In Review

The goal of this chapter is to show you how to streamline lots of decisions into an easy-to-follow SELECT CASE statement. QBasic's SELECT CASE statement executes one of a series of statements based on a certain case matching up.

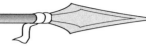

Although you can write equivalent code using IF-ELSE statements inside other IF-ELSE statements, the SELECT CASE statement is easier to follow and makes your programs easier to change later if needed.

The SELECT CASE is especially useful for menu selections.

Code Example

```
PRINT "What would you like to order:"
PRINT "1. Italian food"
PRINT "2. Seafood"
PRINT "3. Health food"
PRINT "4. Mexican food"
PRINT "What is your choice"; ans
SELECT CASE ans
CASE 1 :
   PRINT "Our special is lasagna"
CASE 2 :
   PRINT "Our special is whiting"
CASE 3 :
   PRINT "Our special is grass root pie"
CASE 4 :
   PRINT "Our special is chili verde"
CASE ELSE :
   PRINT "What's the matter, not hungry?"
END SELECT
```

Code Analysis

This SELECT CASE really is implementing a menu! Depending on the user's answer, one of five food messages prints. The CASE ELSE statement handles the condition that sometimes occurs if none of the other CASE values matches that of the SELECT CASE line. Therefore, if the user enters a 7, the last message prints because there is no CASE 7 : statement.

Can I
Repeat Code?

With the DO Loop You Can

This chapter teaches you how to play loop-the-loop with your QBasic programs! A loop is nothing more than a repeated section of a program. You often might want parts of a program to repeat, such as a menu that redisplays after each selection and a payroll program that keeps printing checks for every employee rather than just one per program run.

Loops make your programs powerful. Loops allow a section of a program to execute over and over depending on the data being processed. The only time you do not want to loop is when you accidentally write an *infinite loop.* That is a loop that never stops but keeps repeating forever.

YIKES!

If you accidentally write a program that loops continuously, you can stop the program and return to QBasic's editor by pressing Ctrl+Break.

DO a QBasic Loop

The DO statement begins a loop. There are several forms of the DO loop in QBasic. Following are the formats of two of the most common kinds of QBasic loops. The first one is called the DO WHILE-LOOP:

```
DO WHILE relation
    Block of one or more QBasic statements
LOOP
```

The next loop is called the DO-LOOP WHILE (notice the placement of the WHILE):

```
DO
    Block of one or more QBasic statements
LOOP WHILE relation
```

The *relation* looks exactly like the IF statement's *relation*. The IF and the DO statements have a lot in common. However, instead of performing a set of code *once* as the IF does if the *relation* is true, the DO performs a set of code many times as long as the *relation* is true. Figure 15.1 shows you the action of a DO loop.

Figure 15.1.

Part of a program repeats when a DO's relation is true.

These statements repeat awhile

```
' Short program with a loop
A = 1
DO WHILE (A < 20)
        PRINT "Still counting..."
        A = A + 1
LOOP
PRINT "I'm ending now..."
END
```

HMM...

The body of an IF statement never executes more than once. The body of a loop usually executes more than once.

PSST!

The *relation* tells QBasic when to end the loop. When the *relation* is no longer true, the loop terminates and the rest of the program continues. Therefore, something inside the loop must be able to change the *relation* somehow so that the *relation* eventually becomes false.

The DO WHILE-LOOP

The DO WHILE-LOOP performs its relational test at the top of the loop. Notice that the WHILE *relation* appears before the body of the loop. This means that QBasic tests the *relation* before the loop ever begins and executes the loop the first time only if the *relation* is true. Here is an example program that demonstrates this loop:

```
' Program with a loop
CLS
INPUT "Please enter a letter and I'll speak ASCII... ", ltr$
DO WHILE (ltr$ <> "")
                  ' Keep looping until Enter is only keystroke
   PRINT "The ASCII value of "; ltr$; " is"; ASC(ltr$)
   PRINT "Please enter another letter ";
   INPUT "(Enter by itself ends the program) ", ltr$
LOOP
END    ' Falls through here if just Enter is pressed
```

Here is the output of the program if the user enters a letter three times and then just presses Enter at the fourth prompt:

```
Please enter a letter and I'll speak ASCII... a
The ASCII value of a is 97
Please enter another letter (Enter by itself ends the program) b
The ASCII value of b is 98
Please enter another letter (Enter by itself ends the program) f
The ASCII value of f is 102
Please enter another letter (Enter by itself ends the program)
```

The DO WHILE's body continues executing as long as the *relation* is true. In this program, as long as the user enters a letter, the body of the loop prints the ASCII value of that letter (with the ASC() function). When the user wants to quit, he or she can press Enter without typing a letter. An empty string (empty strings are designated with two quotation marks, "") makes the DO WHILE *relation* false because the *relation* is true only if the user's keystroke is *not* equal to an empty string.

PSST!   It helps to clarify where a loop begins and ends if you indent the body of DO WHILE loops as done here.

You'll find a DO WHILE loop controlling Appendix B's slot machine game. The loop continues letting the player play as long as the total cash is more than $0.00.

The DO-LOOP WHILE

The DO-LOOP WHILE is almost like the DO WHILE-LOOP, with one difference: A DO-LOOP WHILE always executes at least once because the *relation* is at the bottom of the loop. Figure 15.2 indicates where the two kinds of loops test for their continue/stop *relation*.

Figure 15.2.

The two kinds of DO *loops test their relations at different locations.*

YIKES!

If you are still unsure how these two similar-but-different loops work, look at them this way: The first one might not ever execute because the *relation* might be false to begin with. The second one *always* executes at least once.

The following program uses a short number-guessing game to demonstrate the DO-LOOP WHILE and to bring together a lot of the concepts you have learned. The program first generates a random number. The RANDOMIZE TIMER ensures that the internal clock is used to seed the RND function so that the program is different every time you run it. A random number is then generated from 1 to 100 and stored in rnum. The program then loops over and over until the user guesses the number. Notice how IF statements inside the loop provide hints along the way. Also, the variable count is added to each time the user guesses incorrectly. Therefore, count will hold the total number of guesses the user took.

```
' Number-guessing program with count and hints
' Generates a random number for the user to guess
RANDOMIZE TIMER      ' Seed the random-number generator
rnum = INT(RND * 100) + 1    ' Generate a number from 1 to 100
count = 0
CLS
PRINT "I am thinking of a number..."
PRINT
DO
   INPUT "What number am I thinking"; userNum
   IF (userNum > rnum) THEN
      PRINT "Your guess is too high, try again"
   END IF
   IF (userNum < rnum) THEN
      PRINT "Your guess is too low, try again"
   END IF
   count = count + 1     ' Add 1 to the count
LOOP WHILE (rnum <> userNum) ' Keep looping until user guesses
PRINT "Congratulations!"
PRINT "You guessed the number in only"; count; "tries!"
END
```

PSST!   Don't just study the listing. The number-guessing game is most useful if you type it and run it yourself a few times to see how it works.

Happy Hunting

 When you need to execute the same section of a program more than once, don't repeat the same lines back-to-back. Instead, use a DO loop.

 Use either the DO-LOOP WHILE or the DO WHILE-LOOP depending on whether you want the loop to execute at least once or maybe not at all.

 Be sure to do something in the loop to change the *relation* being tested after WHILE, or you'll have an infinite loop on your hands!

Charged

 Don't confuse IF with the DO loops. They both have a *relation*, but the IF *relation* controls only a single set of statements, whereas the DO controls a repeated set of statements.

Fun Fact
There are two more DO loops in QBasic that repeat until a certain condition is met, as opposed to repeating while a certain condition is met. If you want to use these two loops, change your WHILE statements to UNTIL statements in your DO loops. There are so many ways to loop that a person could get loopy!

In Review

The goal of this chapter is to teach you ways to write QBasic loops. A loop repeats a series of one or more QBasic statements while a certain condition is true. The loop must contain a relational test at either the top or the bottom of the loop to end the loop after the condition becomes true.

Code Example

```
i = 1
DO
   PRINT "Repeating..."
   i = i + 1      ' Add 1 to i
WHILE (i <= 5)    ' Loop five times
```

Code Analysis

This section of code prints a message five times. The loop's control variable, i, changes inside the loop. If i were never changed from 1 to something else, the loop could never finish because the WHILE would always be true.

The DO loops are extremely useful for looping while conditions, such as data values being input by the user, are still true. If, however, you ever need to loop a specific number of times, there is a better way, as taught in the next chapter.

How Can
I Specify Better
Loop Control?

Using FOR

 Cycling with **FOR**   146

One of the most popular loop-control statements in QBasic is the FOR loop. A FOR loop allows more control than WHILE loops provide. With a FOR loop you can specify how many times you want to loop, whereas you must continue looping as long as a condition is true with WHILE loops.

There is room for both kinds of loops in QBasic programs. At times, one kind fits a program's requirements better than another. For example, if you wrote a program to handle customer orders as customers purchased items from a store, you would need to use a WHILE loop. The program would process orders *while* customers came through the door. If 100 customers happened to buy items, the WHILE loop would happen to run 100 times. At the end of the day you might want to add the 100 customer purchases to get a total for the day. You could use a FOR loop because you would then know exactly how many times to loop.

HMM... By incrementing counter variables, you can simulate a FOR loop by using WHILE. You can also simulate a WHILE with a FOR! Therefore, the choice of loop you use ultimately depends on which loop you feel most comfortable with at the time you need one. (You saw this in the chapter-ending code of the preceding chapter.)

Cycling with FOR

The FOR loop is important for controlling repeating sections of code. As with DO-LOOP and IF-END IF, a FOR loop spans more than one line and has a closing statement that signals where the end of the FOR loop occurs. This ending statement is the NEXT statement; you never see a FOR without NEXT a few lines later. Here is the format of the FOR statement:

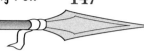

```
FOR counter = start TO end [STEP increment]
    One or more QBasic statements
NEXT counter
```

HMM...

The STEP *increment* is optional because it is enclosed in brackets in the FOR statement's format.

Here is a FOR loop that prints Hi five times:

```
FOR x = 1 TO 5
    PRINT "Hi"
NEXT x
```

The first time through the loop, x is 1. After the body of the loop (the PRINT statement) executes, x becomes 2 and the loop starts over again. When x becomes 5, the PRINT executes one last time. QBasic stops when the *counter* variable becomes more than the *end* value (which is 5 in this FOR loop).

The reason that the loop cycles five times is that the *counter* variable, x, is first assigned a 1, then a 2, and so on until it is finally assigned a 5 by the FOR statement.

PSST!

The body of a FOR loop is usually indented (as all loop bodies should be), and the body can be several statements long if you need it to be.

QBasic's FOR works just like a spoken "for each" statement (that's why it's called FOR!). To gradually ease you into FOR loops, here is a simple loop that explains the FOR and NEXT statements probably better than any other could:

```
' This program prints the numbers 1 through 10
CLS
FOR ctr = 1 TO 10
   PRINT ctr
NEXT ctr
END
```

Here is the output from the program:

```
1
2
3
4
5
6
7
8
9
10
```

Here is the same loop written as a DO WHILE statement:

```
ctr = 1
DO WHILE (ctr <= 10)
   PRINT ctr
   ctr = ctr + 1     ' Add 1 to ctr
LOOP
```

YIKES!

Notice that this WHILE is not as easy to follow as FOR, yet the two loops are equivalent. FOR is best used when a fixed number of repetitions has to be made based on a variable's value.

HMM...

The FOR loop automatically changes its own *counter* variable. When a repetition of the FOR loop ends, QBasic adds the *increment* value to the *counter* variable for you. If you use a DO loop, you have to write the adding statement yourself.

The DO-LOOP WHILE loop cannot substitute for the FOR loop because the *relation* test is performed *before* the body of the FOR loop and after the body of the DO-LOOP WHILE. The DO-LOOP WHILE's test, as you might recall from the end of the preceding chapter, is always at the bottom of the loop.

PSST!

The FOR loop reads a lot like the way you speak in everyday life. Consider this statement:

```
"For each of our 45 employees, calculate the pay and
print a check."
```

This statement leaves no room for ambiguity. There will be 45 employees, 45 pay calculations, and 45 checks printed.

FOR loops don't always count up as the preceding loop did with ctr. Here is a FOR loop that counts down before printing a message:

```
FOR cDown = 10 TO 0 STEP -1
    PRINT cDown
NEXT cDown
PRINT "Blast off!"
```

Here is the output of this code:

```
10
9
8
7
6
5
4
3
2
1
0
Blast off!
```

PSST!   If a FOR loop needs to count down, you must supply a negative STEP value. You don't have to supply a STEP value if the
loop counts up as shown previously, unless the counting
value is to be more than one.

The following FOR loop counts up by threes:

```
FOR i = 1 TO 22 STEP 3    ' The STEP is required!
   PRINT i       ' Prints 1, 4, 7, 10, 13, 16, 19, 22
NEXT i
```

The following code produces an interesting effect:

```
FOR outer = 1 TO 3
   FOR inner = 1 TO 5
      PRINT inner;      ' Leaves the cursor on the same line
   NEXT inner
NEXT outer
                ' Prints 1 2 3 4 5 1 2 3 4 5 1 2 3 4 5
```

If you put a FOR loop in the body of another FOR loop, you are *nesting*
the loops. In effect, the inner loop executes as many times as the
outer loop dictates. You might need a nested FOR loop if you wanted
to print five lists of your top 10 customers. The outer loop moves
from 1 to 5 while the inner loop prints the 10 customers.

An additional statement sometimes comes in handy when you are
working with FOR loops. The EXIT FOR statement quits a FOR loop
earlier than its natural conclusion. Depending on the data, you
might need to stop a FOR loop from executing to its normal comple-
tion. Suppose you wrote a program that asked the user for 20 values
to average (for a teacher with 20 students, for example), but the user
has only 15 values to enter when he or she runs the program (perhaps 5 students were sick). The user could enter -99 for a trigger
value to end the loop early with a statement like this:

```
IF (inputVal = -99) THEN
   EXIT FOR
END IF
```

Happy Hunting

 Use a FOR loop when you want to increment or decrement a variable through a loop.

 Remember that the FOR loop's relational test is performed at the top of the loop.

 Use a nested loop if you want to loop a certain number of times.

 If you need to end a FOR loop early, use an EXIT FOR statement to do so.

Charged

 Don't forget to use STEP if you want the FOR loop to count down (or count up more than one at a time).

 Don't use a *start* value that is greater than the *end* value if you want to count down with FOR.

In Review

The goal of this chapter is to show you how to write FOR loops that execute a fixed number of times. Whereas a WHILE loop might execute one or more times depending on the result of a relational test, a FOR loop executes a fixed number of times as determined by the values and expression following the FOR.

Code Example

```
avg = 0
INPUT "How many numbers do you need to average"; n
FOR i = 1 TO n      ' Loops n times
  INPUT "Enter a number: ", num
  avg = avg + num        ' Add the number to the total
NEXT i                   ' Get another number
avg = avg / n            ' Calculate average
PRINT "The average of your numbers is"; avg
END
```

Code Analysis

This program first asks the user for a number. A FOR loop is then set up to loop using the variable i as the loop's counter variable. i is first assigned the value 1, then the second time through the loop i becomes 2, and so on until i exceeds the user's number.

Each time the body of the loop (the indented statements) executes, the value of the user's newly entered number is added to a total stored in avg. avg began with 0 (at the top of the program) and continues being added to until the FOR loop finishes its job.

Lastly, avg is divided by the number of values entered by the user, and the resulting average is printed.

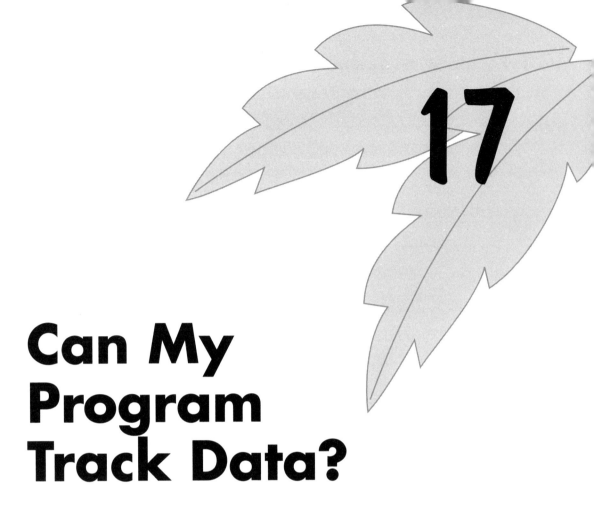

Can My Program Track Data?

The **READ-DATA** Statements Make It Easy

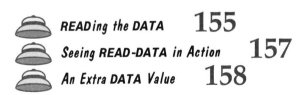

As you write QBasic programs, you will find that you often initialize the same set of variables over and over in more than one program. For example, suppose you write programs for an accounting firm that has four offices located in different quadrants of your city. The offices might be distinguished in reports and on the computer screen by their locations, East, West, North, and South. In every program that deals with the four offices, you'll probably have statements that look something like this:

```
office1$ = "East"
office2$ = "West"
office3$ = "North"
office4$ = "South"
```

The assignments would be more lengthy if there were 10 different office locations rather than only 4.

There is lots of data, such as month names and days of the week, that you will initialize time and again in a lot of different programs. Instead of listing a bunch of assignment statements that take up program space, you can more directly store and assign these data values using READ and DATA statements.

YIKES!

READ and DATA go together—you'll never see a program with one and not the other. Unlike FOR and NEXT and IF and END IF, however, there does not have to be a one-to-one correspondence with READ and DATA. There might be one READ and many DATA statements or the other way around.

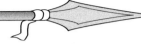

READing the DATA

Use READ and DATA only to fill variables with values you know at the time you write the program. You cannot use READ to initialize a variable with user input—that is the job of INPUT. Here are the formats of the READ and DATA statements:

```
READ variable [, variable] [, variable] [, ..., variable]

DATA literal [, literal] [, literal] [, ..., literal]
```

There can be one or more *variable*s following READ, and there can be one or more *literal*s following DATA. Only variable names follow READ statements, but variable names never follow DATA statements.

PSST!   For a review of the term *literal*, review Chapter 10, "How Do I Specify Different Data?"

HMM...   If you list more than one *variable* or *literal* in a READ or DATA statement, you must separate those variables or literals with commas.

READ and DATA replace a long series of assignment statements. That is their only purpose. Often, it is easier to perform variable assignments using READ and DATA than using the equal sign. The accounting office assignment statements listed in this chapter's introduction can be rewritten using these READ and DATA statements:

```
READ office1$, office2$, office3$, office4$
DATA "East", "West", "North", "South"
```

The data types of the READ variables must match up with the literal data types after DATA. Here is a READ statement that reads both numeric and string variables. The DATA statement lists literals of the same data types. QBasic issues an error if you attempt to run a program in which the DATA types do not match the variables being read with READ.

Figure 17.1 shows how QBasic views the following two statements:

```
READ age%, name$, salary#, weight!
DATA 31, "Victoria Barkley", 425553.10, 116.5
```

Figure 17.1.

The variables after
READ and the
values after DATA
must match in
number and type.

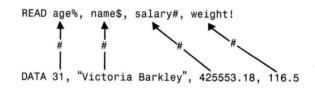

PSST! The DATA can be spaced over several lines. Here is an equivalent set of statements:

```
READ age%, name$, salary#, weight!

DATA 31

DATA "Victoria Barkley", 425553.10

DATA 116.5
```

Skip This, It's Technical

DATA statements are known to be *passive*. That is, they don't actually do anything but hold data that will be read by a READ statement. As QBasic reads data, that data is remembered by QBasic and never read again. Therefore, data values in DATA statements can go anywhere in a program. Some QBasic programmers prefer to put all their DATA statements at the end of the program listing to get the data out of the way, even though READ statements appear throughout the earlier part of the program reading that data. DATA statements can go anywhere before, immediately after, or many lines after the READ statements that read the data. When QBasic encounters a READ, QBasic scans the program looking for *unread* DATA values and assigns the first one found to the variable being read next.

Seeing READ-DATA in Action

Typing a list of READ and DATA statements might seem like just as much work as typing several assignment statements—and it is. The advantage of READ and DATA is that all your data can be in one place and you can change it easier than if you must search through a program looking for assignment statements.

Here is a simple program that uses DATA statements to store a list of values. A loop reads those values one at a time, adding them to produce a total:

```
total = 0        ' No numbers have been added yet
FOR i = 1 TO 8
   READ num
   total = total + num   ' Add the value just read to total
NEXT i
PRINT "The total of the numbers is"; total
DATA 32, 67, 86, 34, 65, 12, 69, 10
```

The following program reads five of the greatest President's first names into variables and then prints the names. Notice that the DATA statement immediately follows the READ statement here. It does not matter where you place a DATA statement.

```
' Program to read and print five names
FOR n = 1 TO 5
   READ pres$        ' Read the next name
   DATA "Thomas", "Abe", "Richard", "Ronald", "George"
   PRINT pres$
NEXT n
END
```

PSST! The READ statement *will not read the same value twice.*

An Extra DATA Value

Many QBasic programmers insert an extra DATA value at the beginning of their DATA statements. The extra value is just a number that indicates how many DATA values follow. You can then add or remove DATA values without worrying about the rest of the program. For example, the following program reads 10 DATA values, totals them, then computes their average. Notice that the first DATA value, 10, is not really DATA, but it tells QBasic exactly how many times the FOR loop is to repeat.

```
' Read and compute DATA based on a count value
READ numData        ' Find out how many data values there are
total = 0           ' Nothing in total yet
FOR c = 1 TO numData
   READ dataValue
   total = total + dataValue    ' Add the data value just read
NEXT c
' Compute the average
avg = total / numData
PRINT "The average of the data is"; avg
DATA 10
DATA 4, 6, 12, 64, 40, 23, 45, 60, 19, 52
END
```

PSST! If you want to add more DATA values, change the first DATA value so that it reflects the count of the items that follow. The rest of the program still works. You truly have data that changes without having to change the program.

Happy Hunting

 Use READ and DATA to assign variables values that are known in advance.

 Put all DATA statements together (the end of program is best) to make them easier to maintain.

 If your DATA changes frequently, consider controlling the DATA with a count value. If you add or remove DATA values, you only have to change the count.

Charged

 Don't mix data types. READing a string value into a numeric variable is just as wrong as trying to assign a string to a numeric variable.

In Review

The goal of this chapter is to explain READ and DATA statements. The READ statement reads values into variables. READ gets its values from DATA statements that appear elsewhere in the program. The command READ is always followed by variable names, and DATA is always followed by constant data values.

The DATA statement or statements don't have to be next to their corresponding READ statements. DATA statements are passive; they don't do anything by themselves. READ will search for DATA no matter where the DATA statements reside in the program.

Code Example

```
READ checkRate
READ savRate
PRINT "The checking account rate is"; checkRate
PRINT "The savings account rate is"; savRate
DATA .07, .085
```

Code Analysis

This code reads two values into checking-account and savings-account interest rate variables. Both of the READ statement's values are stored in a single DATA statement. You don't have to have a corresponding READ for every DATA or vice versa. As long as there are enough DATA values following DATA to fill all the program's READ variables, the program will work fine.

The DATA statement could appear anywhere in the code's program, and the program would work without any different result. The data in DATA statements is easy to change because all the program's data appears in the same section of the program if you group your DATA statements together.

Part V
Lots of Lists, Tables, and Storage

"I'd give you a ride if I had room, old boy!
I bet you hear that all the time!"

Can QBasic Deal with Lists?

Use Arrays for That

An *array* is a list of variables. Not just any variables, but special kinds of variables called *array variables.* Any of QBasic's data types can be turned into an array if you need to keep track of lots of values. Compared with the stand-alone variables you have read about so far, array variables are much easier to work with. You don't have to give each variable in the array list a different name. Instead, the entire array of variables has a single name.

Before getting too much further into arrays, you could use an overview: If you ever want to store lots of data, such as 100 employee names, 35 student grades, 500 inventory items, or 1,000 checks you've written over the past year, it is much easier to use an array than to use a bunch of differently named variables.

HMM...   Each of the variables in an array list is called an *element.* Therefore, if you store 100 names in a string array, you simply have 100 elements, each of which is different, but all 100 elements are the same data type (strings).

Defining Arrays

When you work with several non-array variables, you have to assign each a different name. If you wrote a program to keep track of your monthly household expense total, you might use variable names such as these:

expense1   expense2   expense3   expense4   expense5

Instead of keeping track of lots of variable names, you should use an array. Unlike with regular variables, with an array you have to tell QBasic near the top of a program that you'll need an array. In other words, you don't have to tell QBasic that you need a variable named

expense1 because it is a regular non-array variable; you can just start using it. However, before using an array, you have to tell QBasic that you'll need one.

The DIM statement tells QBasic that you'll need an array later in the program. DIM tells QBasic the name of the array and how many elements are in it. Only after including the DIM can you use the array. Here is the format of DIM:

```
DIM arrayName(numElements) [ , arrayName(numElements)...]
```

PSST! DIM comes from the word *dimension*.

The following statement reserves eight array elements. You know the array is single-precision because all variables that have no data-type suffixes are single-precision, as you learned in Chapter 10, "How Do I Specify Different Data?" A picture of the array as it is stored in memory is shown in Figure 18.1.

```
DIM amounts(8)    ' Reserve 8 array elements
```

Figure 18.1.

The eight dimensioned array elements and their subscripts.

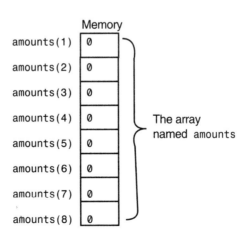

PSST!   Each array element in Figure 18.1 has a zero because QBasic always zeroes out all variables. Array elements are variables stored as a list.

Each array element has a *subscript,* a number in parentheses. The subscript differentiates each array element from the other array elements. Because the array elements are differentiated by a subscript value rather than a different variable name, you can use a FOR loop to scan through the array (printing the array, totaling it, or whatever else you might want to do with the values).

HMM...   Notice that each subscript is enclosed in parentheses.

Skip This, It's Technical

QBasic does reserve an element with the subscript 0, but most QBasic programmers start with the subscript 1 instead. Beginning the array at subscript 0 means that an array you dimension as 8 actually has 9 elements (with the subscripts 0 through 8).

Using Arrays

You will use arrays to keep track of lots of data. You can ask the user for lots of values, store those values in an array, and then print those values in any order you want. Array elements are variables that you distinguish from each other with subscripts. Following is

a short program that dimensions 20 array elements, reads the numbers into the array from DATA statements, and then prints the array backward. Because you can reference an array in any order, the FOR loop prints the array backward.

```
' Reads values into an array and prints them backward
DIM vals(20)
' Read the array values
FOR i = 1 TO 20
   READ vals(i)
NEXT i
' Print the array backward
PRINT "Here is the array:"
FOR i = 20 TO 1 STEP -1
   PRINT vals(i)
NEXT i
DATA 10, 41, 34, 93, 29, 30, 73, 88, 4, 12
DATA 65, 34, 70, 41, 23, 41, 16, 52, 44, 34
END
```

HMM...

Here would be a nice exercise to test your array forte: Add some code to this program that totals the array as you read each value, then prints the total after all the array elements are printed.

Suppose you wanted to write a program to keep track of a company's inventory. Although the program shown next still has room for improvement (a true inventory program needs to be able to store values in a disk file and print listings to the printer), the program presents a good start toward improving your understanding of arrays.

```
' Inventory program that uses arrays
' Room for up to 50 inventory items
DIM prodCode$(50)
DIM desc$(50)
DIM price!(50)
DIM quant%(50)
numItems = 0 ' Inventory count
```

```
' Get all the inventory items from the user
CLS
FOR numItems = 1 TO 50
  PRINT
  PRINT "What is the next product code"
  INPUT "(Press Enter to stop entering)"; prodCode$(numItems)
  IF (prodCode$(numItems) <> "") THEN
    INPUT "What is the item's description"; desc$(numItems)
    INPUT "What is the item's price"; price!(numItems)
    INPUT "What is the item's quantity"; quant%(numItems)
  ELSE
    numItems = numItems - 1 ' Don't increment count after all
    EXIT FOR
  END IF
NEXT numItems
' Print the listing on the screen
PRINT
PRINT "Here is an inventory listing:"
FOR cnt = 1 TO numItems
  PRINT
  PRINT "Product Code: "; prodCode$(cnt)
  PRINT "Description: "; desc$(cnt)
  PRINT "Price:"; price!(cnt)
  PRINT "Quantity:"; quant%(cnt)
NEXT cnt
END
```

Here is sample output from the program. Although only 3 inventory items are entered and printed here, the program's array size leaves room for up to 50.

```
What is the next product code
(Press Enter to stop entering)? 1A2C-7
What is the item's description? Wedge Widgets
What is the item's price? 2.13
What is the item's quantity? 47

What is the next product code
(Press Enter to stop entering)? 4G5S-9
What is the item's description? Bolts (small)
What is the item's price? .32
What is the item's quantity? 165

What is the next product code
(Press Enter to stop entering)? 7T5W-0
What is the item's description? Bolts (large)
```

```
What is the item's price? .54
What is the item's quantity? 490

What is the next product code
(Press Enter to stop entering)?

Here is an inventory listing:

Product Code: 1A2C-7
Description: Wedge Widgets
Price: 2.13
Quantity: 47

Product Code: 4G5S-9
Description: Bolts (small)
Price: .32
Quantity: 165

Product Code: 7T5W-0
Description: Bolts (large)
Price: .54
Quantity: 490
```

Happy Hunting

 Use arrays when you want to store lots of values of the same data type.

 Put the array's data type suffix in front of the subscript's parentheses.

 Use a FOR loop to step through each element of your array.

Charged

 Don't forget to dimension enough elements for your arrays.

In Review

The goal of this chapter is to teach you how to store lists of values in array variables. An array is just a list of variables. Instead of having different names, the variables in the array, called elements, are differentiated by a numeric subscript.

Before you can use an array in a QBasic program, you must reserve storage for the array with a DIM statement. DIM comes from the word *dimension.*

Code Example

```
DIM seasons$(4)           ' Reserve storage
FOR i = 1 TO 4
   READ seasons$(i)       ' Store a season name in the array
NEXT i
DATA "Winter"
DATA "Spring"
DATA "Summer"
DATA "Fall"
PRINT "The first season is "; seasons$(1)
PRINT "The second season is "; seasons$(2)
PRINT "The third season is "; seasons$(3)
PRINT "The fourth season is "; seasons$(4)
END
```

Code Analysis

This program reserves a four-element string array named seasons$ that hold the names of the four seasons. The season names are read into the array using READ and DATA statements and then are printed.

With only four names, an array is not really necessary, but the seasons$ array does provide a nice storage bin for the data.

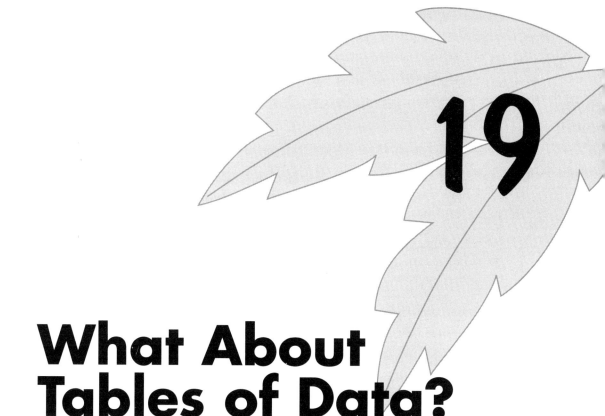

What About Tables of Data?

QBasic Offers Matrix Control

Some data fits better in a *matrix* than in an array. A matrix is nothing more than a *table* of values, whereas an array is just a list of values. Often, QBasic programmers call matrices *tables* rather than *matrices* because a table better describes the look of matrix data. Not all data fits in a matrix format. It might be a while before you use matrices, but they are handy when you need them.

There is very little in this chapter that you did not learn about in the preceding chapter. Matrices have subscripts. A matrix is a table of variables, and each variable is called an *element*. The table has one name, and the individual elements are differentiated by their subscripts.

HMM...   The primary difference between matrices and arrays is their layout in memory. A matrix (table) has both rows and columns, and therefore each matrix element has *two* subscripts, one for the row and one for the column of the element.

Dimensioning Arrays

Suppose you needed to write a program to keep track of your annual salary. You wouldn't need an array because there is only one value to track! However, what if you wanted to keep each month's pay stored so that you could print any or all of the amounts? An array of 12 values would be perfect for that purpose. Now, what if you wanted to keep track of *five years'* worth of those monthly payroll values? A matrix is perfect for that.

Here is the DIM statement that would reserve five years' worth of 12 monthly values:

```
DIM myPay(5, 12)    ' Reserve 5 years worth of monthly payroll
```

Figure 19.1 shows you the table generated by this DIM statement. The DIM statement for tables always includes two subscripts, one for the rows and one for the columns.

Figure 19.1.

Looking at the format of the myPay matrix.

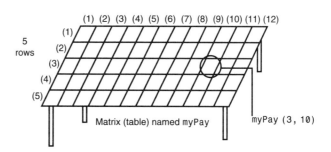

PSST! The first subscript indicates the rows, and the second one indicates columns. The myPay matrix contains 60 elements ranging from myPay(1,1) to myPay(5,12).

The following assignment statements put values in some of myPay's elements:

```
myPay(2, 1) = 4124.34    ' The 2nd year, 1st month
myPay(3, 5) = 2438.52    ' The 3rd year, 5th month
myPay(3, 12) = 5234.29   ' The 3rd year, 12th month
myPay(4, 6) = 6952.12    ' The 4th year, 6th month
```

Of course, instead of assigning individual matrix values, your programs will usually loop and ask the user for the values or read them from DATA (or read them from a disk file, as you'll learn how to do in the next chapter).

YIKES!

Matrix variables can have data type suffixes just like any other kind of variables. The data type suffix goes just before the left parenthesis, like this: `myPay#(2, 3)` or `names$(5, 1)`.

Using Matrices

Nested `FOR` loops are perfect for stepping through matrices. For instance, the outer loop can control the rows (in `myPay`, the row numbers would go from 1 to 5), and the inner loop can control the columns (in `myPay`, the column numbers would go from 1 to 12). The following section of code dimensions a matrix named `values` to 3 rows and 7 columns, then assigns a 25 to each value in the matrix. (Why you would want to do *that* is a mystery to both of us!)

```
DIM values(3, 7)
FOR rows = 1 TO 3
   FOR cols = 1 TO 7
      values(rows, cols) = 25
   NEXT cols
NEXT rows
```

YIKES!

Remember that a nested `FOR` loop is a loop within a loop. The `rows` variable steps through each row while the inner loop makes the `cols` variable step "across" each column in the row.

PSST!

Using a nested FOR loop for initializing and printing a table might be made even clearer if you saw the row and cols variables printed as done here:

```
FOR rows = 1 TO 3
   FOR cols = 1 TO 7
      PRINT rows; TAB(5); cols
   NEXT cols
NEXT rows
```

Here are the first few lines of output (you can figure out the rest):

```
1    1
1    2
1    3
1    4
1    5
1    6
1    7
2    1
2    2
2    3
```

Think of these printed numbers as the table's subscripts, and you'll see why a nested loop is perfect for stepping through every element in a table.

Let's Write a Program

Perhaps a step-by-step building of a program might further explain the use of tables. Suppose you wanted to write a program that printed a report for a home mail-order business. The mail-order business sells five different sets of stationery. Because of inventory control, you want to print a report showing how each set's sales compares with the other's. The sets are named Bright Birds, Fun Flowers, Krazy Kids, Colorful Creation, and Thanx-a-Lot.

The report will be printed at the end of each month, and you'll want each week's sales printed by stationery set. In other words, the report will show a table with five columns, one column for each set of stationery. The table will have four rows, one row for each week. You can dimension the table like this:

```
DIM cards(4, 5)    ' 4 rows, 5 columns
```

Instead of prompting the user for the 20 values every time the report is printed, the program should read the 20 values from DATA statements. Each month, the DATA statements can change so a new report is generated.

 PSST!   Even better would be the storage of the data on disk, as you'll learn in the next chapter.

The following code would read the 20 data values for the card's sales into the table:

```
FOR week = 1 TO 4
    FOR set = 1 TO 5
        READ cards(week, set)
    NEXT set
NEXT week
DATA 425.64, 342.34, 132.67, 592.00, 352.67
DATA 294.21, 291.10, 183.93, 452.46, 368.19
DATA 381.45, 523.45, 132.30, 432.12, 425.53
DATA 317.66, 343.45, 423.54, 311.44, 685.21
```

After the data is read, it is time to print a nice-looking report. Of course, you should label the columns and rows. The following LPRINT statements would be perfect for the stationery set names across the top of each column:

```
LPRINT "        Bright    Fun     Krazy    Colorful   Thanx-"
LPRINT "        Birds   Flowers   Kids     Creation    a-lot"
```

In a moment you'll see why the extra space was left before the titles.

The data values now must be printed. You'll want to space the values properly so that they print under the titles. Also, the week number at the beginning of each row would be helpful. Try to figure out how the following statements would produce the data:

```
FOR week = 1 TO 4
   PRINT "Week"; week;     ' Leave a trailing cursor
   FOR set = 1 TO 5
                    ' Ensure that 4 blanks print after numbers
      PRINT USING "###.##     "; cards(week, set);
   NEXT set
   PRINT    ' At end of each row, move cursor down to next line
NEXT week
```

You want Week 1, Week 2, and so on only at the *start* of each line. Therefore, those labels should print only inside the outer loop, not after the inner loop prints each number. To keep the numbers aligned, a PRINT USING was used. A trailing semicolon is left at the end of each value printed so that the *next* value prints on that same line. After all five columns have printed, a PRINT residing on a single line moves the cursor down to start the next row.

Finally, a total of each stationery set would be helpful to show which set sells the most. Only five totals are needed, one for each set. Another array of five values would be helpful here. The following code would dimension the array and total each of the five sets:

```
DIM totals(5)
totals(1) = cards(1, 1) + cards(2, 1) + cards(3, 1) + cards(4, 1)
totals(2) = cards(1, 2) + cards(2, 2) + cards(3, 2) + cards(4, 2)
totals(3) = cards(1, 3) + cards(2, 3) + cards(3, 3) + cards(4, 3)
totals(4) = cards(1, 4) + cards(2, 4) + cards(3, 4) + cards(4, 4)
totals(5) = cards(1, 5) + cards(2, 5) + cards(3, 5) + cards(4, 5)
```

If you study the subscripts being used in the totaling, you might see how a nested loop would make the totaling easier. Although the following code doesn't take a lot less typing, the nested loops do make the code easier to maintain if more weeks are needed later:

```
FOR sets = 1 TO 5
   FOR week = 1 TO 4
      totals(sets) = totals(sets) + cards(week, sets)
   NEXT week
NEXT sets
```

Putting all these pieces together produces the following program. Comments and underlining add the finishing touches. Below the program, the output is shown so that you'll be able to trace what is going on.

```
' Program that prints a report showing a mail-order stationery
' business's monthly sales, broken down by week and set
CLS
DIM cards(4, 5), totals(5)
' Read the data
FOR week = 1 TO 4
   FOR set = 1 TO 5
      READ cards(week, set)
   NEXT set
NEXT week
' Total the five sets
FOR sets = 1 TO 5
   FOR week = 1 TO 4
      totals(sets) = totals(sets) + cards(week, sets)
   NEXT week
NEXT sets
' Print a report
LPRINT "      Bright    Fun    Krazy    Colorful   Thanx-"
LPRINT "      Birds   Flowers  Kids    Creation   a-lot"
FOR week = 1 TO 4
   LPRINT "Week"; week;   ' Leave a trailing cursor
   FOR set = 1 TO 5
                      ' Ensure that 4 blanks print after numbers
```

```
        LPRINT USING "###.##     "; cards(week, set);
    NEXT set
    LPRINT   ' At end of each row, move cursor down to next line
NEXT week
LPRINT "        ------    ------    ------    ------    ------"
LPRINT "     ";
FOR i = 1 TO 5
    LPRINT USING "####,.##   "; totals(i);
NEXT i
DATA 425.64, 342.34, 132.67, 592.00, 352.67
DATA 294.21, 291.10, 183.93, 452.46, 368.19
DATA 381.45, 523.45, 132.30, 432.12, 425.53
DATA 317.66, 343.45, 423.54, 311.44, 685.21
END
```

Here is the program's output:

```
           Bright       Fun      Krazy   Colorful    Thanx-
           Birds     Flowers      Kids   Creation    a-lot
Week 1 425.64      342.34    132.67     592.00    352.67
Week 2 294.21      291.10    183.93     452.46    368.19
Week 3 381.45      523.45    132.30     432.12    425.53
Week 4 317.66      343.45    423.54     311.44    685.21
           ------    ------    ------    ------    ------
        1,418.96  1,500.34    872.44  1,788.02  1,831.60
```

YIKES!

Doesn't the output look nice? The table presented here is typical of many report programs. The program is a little tough, but not impossible to figure out. Spending some time learning exactly how this program operates will pay dividends later!

Happy Hunting

Use two-dimensional tables (also called *matrices*) when you have data that fits into a row-and-column format.

A nested FOR loop is perfect when you need to step through all the elements in a matrix.

 Be sure to use two subscripts when you dimension a matrix.

Charged

 Don't confuse the QBasic *matrix* with the mathematical term *matrix*. A QBasic matrix is nothing more than an array that appears in row/column order. Nothing extra is required to work with QBasic matrices than what you already know.

In Review

The goal of this chapter is to extend your knowledge of arrays by showing you how to reserve and use multidimensional arrays. A multidimensional array, called a matrix, has more than one subscript. The values in a matrix form a table (not just a list) that has rows and columns. You must specify two subscripts in a matrix, one for the row number and one for the column number.

Code Example

```
DIM weights(3, 3) ' Reserve a matrix with 3 rows and columns
FOR month = 1 TO 3    ' The rows represent months
   FOR people = 1 TO 3  ' The columns hold people's weights
      READ (month, people)  ' Fill the matrix with weights
   NEXT people
NEXT month
DATA 135, 124, 122
DATA 189, 176, 184
DATA 120, 121, 113
```

Code Analysis

This code reads three people's weights, over a three-month period, into a matrix named `weights`. The matrix has three rows and three columns. Each row represents each of the three people's weights over the three month period.

Nested `FOR-NEXT` loops are useful for initializing and printing matrix variables.

Can I Save to the Disk?

Sure, with Sequential Disk I/O

Be proud! The commands that you are learning are powerful, and the skills you are building will be well rewarded when you write programs for yourself and others. There is, however, one piece of the pie that you still need to understand: how to read from and write to disk files. The disk is semipermanent; after you write data to a disk, that data stays there until you change or delete it.

Until now, you had to either save the program's data in DATA statements or prompt the user with INPUT every time the program was run. There are drawbacks to both methods: If the data changes, you don't want the user to have to change DATA statements because the user of your programs knows nothing about READ, DATA, variables, and the like. In addition, you don't want to get calls in the middle of the night from some user wanting you to come over and change the DATA statements. The second method of getting data into the program, through INPUT statements, is still important, but after the user enters his or her data, that user doesn't want to reenter the same data every time the program is run.

The solution is to use disk files. After you get data from the user with INPUT statements, you can save the data to the disk. Other programs can then read that data from the disk and print or change it as needed. Figure 20.1 helps show the importance of disk files to the long-term storage of your data.

Figure 20.1.

You can make your short-term variables last by storing them on disk.

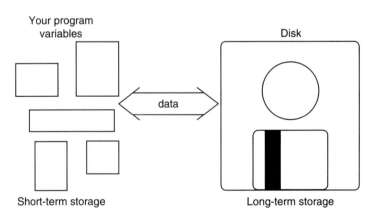

Types of Disk Access

There are two methods QBasic uses to store data on disks: *sequential access* and *random access.* This chapter explores sequential access. The difference between the two methods is this: Sequential-access files must be read in the same order in which they were written to. Not all data fits within a sequential file. For instance, a history of sales would make a good sequential file because the data would be stored in the file in the order the sales were made. However, a parts inventory would not make good sequential file data because you want to be able to access any part in the inventory regardless of when the item was entered in the inventory.

Fun Fact
A disk holds magnetic data just like a cassette tape. You can even store music on your disk drive with today's multimedia computers.

YIKES!

Another advantage that random-access files have over sequential-access files is that you can change random-access files without re-creating the entire file. If you want to change a sequential-access file, you must rewrite the entire file with the new change and delete the old file.

Opening the File Drawer

Before you can read from or write to a file, you must open the file. When you are done with a disk file, you must close the file. Opening the file attaches a *filenumber* to a filename. After you open a file and attach that number, you will then use the number rather than the filename in the rest of the program.

Opening a disk file is analogous to opening a file cabinet drawer. You must open the drawer before you can access a file in the cabinet. You must open a disk file before you can access it. Always close a disk file when you no longer need to access it, or QBasic might lose some of the last few characters you wrote to the disk. (You should close the cabinet drawer when you are done with it too, or you might hit your head!)

Skip This, It's Technical

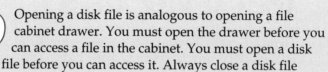

Opening and closing disk files actually cause QBasic to do a lot of work behind the scenes. When you open a file, QBasic makes sure there is room on the disk and in the disk directory for the file. QBasic also makes sure that the filename you specify is valid and does some other important disk housekeeping chores, as well as error-checking. Closing disk files forces QBasic to write the last remaining data to the disk (the data might be stored in a memory *buffer*, or temporary holding area until you close the file) and update the disk directory.

Here is the format of the OPEN statement:

```
OPEN filename$ FOR mode AS [#]filenumber
```

The `filename$` is a string containing a valid filename. If you understand drives and directories, you can specify a complete pathname before the filename. The `mode` is a value from Table 20.1. The `filenumber` (notice that the pound sign is optional) is a number from 1 to 255 that you attach to an open file.

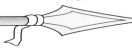

PSST! If you open three files, you'll probably use 1, 2, and 3 for the three files in their corresponding OPEN statements.

Table 20.1. **The QBasic sequential mode values.**

mode	Description
OUTPUT	Used for writing data to a file. If the file already exists, QBasic overwrites the file. If the file does not exist, QBasic creates the file.
APPEND	Used for adding (*appending*) data to a file. If the file already exists, QBasic directs the output from your program to the end of the file. If the file does not exist, QBasic creates the file.
INPUT	Used for reading data from a file. The file you are opening to read should first exist. If the file does not exist when you attempt to open it for input, QBasic issues an error message.

Suppose you wanted to create a sequential file to store your checkbook data. Here is an OPEN statement that would do so:

```
OPEN "checks.dat" FOR OUTPUT AS #1
```

If you wanted to add to the check file, you would write an OPEN statement that looked like this:

```
OPEN "checks.dat" FOR APPEND AS #1
```

PSST! If other files were open when you opened the checks.dat file, you would pick a different *filenumber* if the 1 was already taken by another open file in the program.

To read the file in a program, you would open it like this:

```
OPEN "checks.dat" FOR INPUT AS #1
```

Closing files is easy. Here is the format of the CLOSE statement:

```
CLOSE [[#]filenumber] [, ..., [#]filenumber]
```

You can close a file attached to *filenumber* 1 like this:

```
CLOSE #1
```

You can close three files, each attached to the first three *filenumber*s, in a single CLOSE like this:

```
CLOSE #1, #2, #3
```

Creating a File

The WRITE # statement is a perfect statement to use for writing to a sequential disk file. WRITE # writes both string and numeric variables to a disk file, putting quotation marks around string data and separating all the data values in the file with commas. This makes the data easy to read with a mirror-image INPUT #. Here is the format of WRITE #:

```
WRITE #filenumber data [..., data]
```

And here is the format of INPUT #:

```
INPUT #filenumber data [..., data]
```

Following is a program that writes some words and numbers to the disk:

```
' If you don't have a hard disk, change the C:
' to another drive
OPEN "c:\outfile.dat" FOR OUTPUT AS #1
WRITE #1, "Michael W.", 14, 87.5
```

```
WRITE #1, "Mary C.", 15, 94.1
WRITE #1, "Jack R.", 13, 76.7
CLOSE #1    ' Always close a file when you are done
END
```

PSST! You can specify the filename in either uppercase or lower-case letters.

Here is a listing of the disk file created with this program:

```
"Michael W.",14,87.5
"Mary C.",15,94.1
"Jack R.",13,76.7
```

Reading Files

Reading a sequential data file that you created is almost as easy as writing it. There is only one additional job you must take care of. Most of the time, you'll set up a loop to read values from a file and print or process the values as you read them. Unless you know exactly how many records a file contains, you run the risk of reading past the end of the file.

QBasic supplies the EOF() function, which becomes true if you just read the end of the file. EOF() requires the *filenumber* of the file you are reading in EOF()'s parentheses. EOF() returns a -1 if the end of the file is reached.

YIKES!

Yes, -1 is a strange return value, but that's the way EOF() works. The next program shows you how to read a sequential file and stop when you get to the end of the file.

```
' If you don't have a hard disk, change the
' C: to another drive
CLS
' Print titles on the screen
PRINT "Name"; TAB(16); "Age"; TAB(31); "Score"
OPEN "c:\outfile.dat" FOR INPUT AS #1
' Read and print until you reach the end of file
DO
   INPUT #1, name$, age, score
   PRINT name$; TAB(15); age; TAB(30); score
LOOP WHILE EOF(1) <> -1    ' EOF(1) returns -1 at end-of-file
CLOSE #1    ' Always close a file when you are done
END
```

Here is the output from the program:

```
Name          Age          Score
Michael W.    14           87.5
Mary C.       15           94.1
Jack R.       13           76.7
```

Adding to a File

If you want to add to the end of a sequential file, you can do so by using the APPEND file *access* keyword. After you open a file for APPEND, subsequent WRITE # statements add data to the file. The following program adds two names to the data file created and read in the previous sections:

```
' If you don't have a hard disk, change the
' C: to another drive
CLS
OPEN "c:\outfile.dat" FOR APPEND AS #1  ' Adds to end of file
WRITE #1, "Linda P.", 13, 80.3
WRITE #1, "Ron H.", 14, 99.1
CLOSE #1    ' Always close a file when you are done
END
```

Here is the file after the new lines are added:

```
"Michael W.",14,87.5
"Mary C.",15,94.1
"Jack R.",13,76.7
"Linda P.",13,80.3
"Ron H.",14,99.1
```

Happy Hunting

 Store data in disk files for long-term storage.

 Open all files before you use them, and close them when you are through.

 You can create, add to, and read sequential files.

Charged

 Don't create a sequential file if you ever need to go back and change or reference individual data within the file. Use random-access files for files that change often.

 Don't read past the end of a file. Use EOF() so that you'll know when your program reads the last line in a file.

In Review

The goal of this chapter is to show you how QBasic stores data on the disk drive in sequential files. A sequential file is easy to create, read, and write. Storing data in a disk file requires that you first open the file. Opening a disk file lets QBasic know the name of the file and also how you want to access the file.

You can access a sequential file in one of three ways: read, write, and append. When you read a file, the data in the file loads from the disk into your program's variables. When you write to a file, the data in your program's variables go to the disk file. When you append to a disk, you add data to data that is already there.

Code Example

```
OPEN "c:\cities.dat" FOR OUTPUT AS #1
WRITE #1, "Cairo", 15000000&   ' Long integers
WRITE #1, "Tulsa", 420500&
WRITE #1, "Auckland", 3000000&
CLOSE #1
```

Code Analysis

This program opens a sequential file named cities.dat on the C: disk drive. The file is a sequential file and is created due to the FOR OUTPUT clause of the OPEN statement.

The names and populations of three cities are written to the file, and then the file is closed.

How Can I Do More with the Disk?

Use Random Disk I/O

A random-access file works just like a big array that is stored on your disk. After you store a random-access file, you can access any line in that file randomly. For instance, you can read a random file backward, read every other line, or change only a little of the file's data without rewriting the entire file, and lots more.

The only requirement of random files is that the data within the files have a uniform appearance. For instance, you wouldn't want to store a lot of text, such as sentences, in random files, but inventory data, people's information, and just about any other kind of data that is duplicated in the same format makes good candidate data for random-access files.

PSST!  The lines in a random-access file are called *records*. Each line in a random-access file must be of the same format. If the first record has an integer followed by a string followed by a single-precision value, every record in the file also has to have the same format.

Creating Randomly

Suppose you wanted to write a program for your child that kept track of a comic book collection. Your child would want certain information tracked for each comic. He or she would want each comic's title, date, price, and condition stored in the file. Here is a sample of some comic book data that fits this format:

```
SuperCat       11-09-76 0.25 Fair
Atom Andy      01-22-93 1.25 Good
Hero Harry     07-30-90 0.95 Excellent
Nellie Nurse   08-24-89 0.85 Poor
Computer Thom  12-01-92 1.25 Excellent
```

PSST! Can you see that there are five records in the data just shown? Each record has four columns. A column in a random-access file is called a *field.* Each field is always a uniform width (therefore, assume that spaces pad the right of the comics' conditions shown here).

Random-access files require a special OPEN statement, which takes this format:

```
OPEN filename$ FOR RANDOM AS [#]filenumber LEN=recordLngth
```

The LEN=*recordLngth* is new to you. A sequential file's records each can be different lengths, so you don't have to specify a record length for sequential files. With random files, you must tell the OPEN statement exactly how many memory locations the record takes.

YIKES!

You do not know how to determine the record length of data yet, but the next section shows you a quick way.

Closing random-access files is no different from closing sequential files. The CLOSE for each is the same.

TYPE Your Random Data First

Before you can write or read a random-access file, you must describe to QBasic *exactly* how each record will look. In other words, you must define the *record format*. Use the TYPE statement to define a random-access file's records. Here is the format of the TYPE statement:

```
TYPE recordName
   fieldname AS type
  [...fieldname AS type]
END TYPE
```

The *recordName* is a name that you give to the format (the look) of the record. The AS lines describe each field in the record. The *type* is one of the values from Table 21.1.

Table 21.1. **The type values for the TYPE statement.**

type	Description
STRING * *n*	A string of *n* length
INTEGER	Integer
LONG	Long integer
SINGLE	Single-precision
DOUBLE	Double-precision
Type	Another data type you have already defined with another TYPE statement

An example TYPE statement for the comic book program might look like this:

```
TYPE comicRec
   title     AS STRING * 15
   comDate   AS STRING * 8
   price     AS SINGLE
   condition AS STRING * 9
END TYPE
```

Notice that no data type suffixes are needed on the field names. The AS clause describes the field type and eliminates the need for a suffix.

PSST!

AS STRING specifies the *longest* string length, specified by STRING * *n*, you'll need. All string fields must be large enough to accommodate the largest string you'll ever store there.

Remember the LEN() function? LEN() (as you read in Chapter 12, "Can QBasic Do Much with Strings?") computes and returns the length of the data you put in the parentheses. However, LEN() is not just for string data—LEN() works on records also. Therefore, at the top of the program that tracked the comic book collection, you would put the previous TYPE command, then open the file like this:

```
OPEN "c:\comics.dat" FOR RANDOM AS #1 LEN=LEN(comicRec)
```

YIKES!

TYPE only describes the *format* of a record. You still have to define record variables which take on that format.

Defining a Record Variable

One last step is required before you can write to or read from a random-access file. You must define a record variable. Until this point, all your variables were string, integer, long integer, single-precision, or double-precision. A record variable is an *aggregate variable data type.* A record variable is a variable that looks like the record you define with TYPE.

An extended form of DIM reserves record variables. Here is the format of this new kind of DIM:

```
DIM recordVar AS recordName [,..., recordVar AS recordName]
```

YIKES!

Don't let the keyword DIM throw you. Record variables are not arrays. They are variables that take on several data types according to the format of the TYPE statement.

The following statement reserves three comic book variables that look like the variables in Figure 21.1:

```
DIM comic1 AS comicRec, comic2 AS comicRec, comic3 AS comicRec
```

Figure 21.1.

After three record variables have been defined.

YIKES!

What if there are *400* comic books to track? You don't want 400 different variable names. You can dimension an array of record variables. The following statement does just that:

```
DIM comics(400) AS comicRec ' 400 occurrences of the record
```

The *dot operator* (which is just a period, .) enables you to store values in specific fields within a record variable. For instance, to store the date 01-22-93 in the date field of comic2, you *can't* do this:

```
comic2 = "01-22-93"    ' INVALID since comic2 is a
                       ' record variable
```

comic2 is a record variable, not a string variable. To move down to the date field of comic2, you *can* do this:

```
comic2.comDate = "01-22-93"    ' OK
```

If the comics were stored in an array named comics, you could assign the second element a date like this:

```
comics[2].comDate = "01-22-93"    ' OK
```

Working with the File Data

After you fill a record variable with values, through assignment, INPUT, or READ-DATA, you are ready to write the record variable to the disk. The PUT # statement writes random records. Here is the format of PUT:

```
PUT [#]filenumber, [recordNumber,] , recordVariable
```

The opposite of PUT # is GET #. Often, a mirror-image GET # reads data that was written to a file with PUT #. Here is the format of GET #:

```
GET [#]filenumber, [recordNumber,] , recordVariable
```

The *recordNumber* is a value that works in the file just like a subscript works in arrays. For instance, if you wanted to read the 65th record in a file, you could do so like this:

```
GET #1, 65, comicsBook
```

PSST! If you do not specify a *recordNumber* (it is optional for both GET # and PUT #), QBasic reads or writes to the record following the last record accessed. You must still include two commas if you do not use a *recordNumber* in either the GET # or the PUT #.

The following program asks the user for a comic book's data, then writes (with PUT) that data to a random-access file. A series of GET statements then reads the file, and LPRINT prints the file to the printer.

HMM... Typically, one program collects user input and saves it to the file. Another then reports that file's data. Another might enable the user to change one of the file's records (using techniques you'll read about in the next section).

```
' Program to manage a comic book inventory
TYPE comicRec
    title     AS STRING * 15
    comDate   AS STRING * 8
    price     AS SINGLE
    condition AS STRING * 9
END TYPE
' Only 1 record variable needed because we'll write just
' as soon as the user fills up the record variable
DIM comic AS comicRec
CLS
PRINT "** C o m i c   B o o k   T r a c k e r **"
PRINT
OPEN "c:\comics.dat" FOR RANDOM AS #1 LEN = LEN(comic)
DO
    PRINT "What is the next comic's title?"
    INPUT "(Press Enter to end the input...) ", Ent$
    IF (Ent$ <> "") THEN
        comic.title = Ent$
        INPUT "What is the date of the comic"; comic.comDate
        INPUT "What is the price of the comic"; comic.price
        INPUT "What is the comic's condition"; comic.condition
        PRINT
        PUT #1, , comic   ' Puts at the next record
    END IF
LOOP WHILE (Ent$ <> "")
CLOSE #1    ' This close is not really needed since we're going
            ' to read the same file randomly anyway
' Write a report
LPRINT
LPRINT "Comic Book Inventory"
LPRINT
OPEN "c:\comics.dat" FOR RANDOM AS #1 LEN = LEN(comic)
numRecs = LOF(1) / LEN(comic)
FOR recs = 1 TO numRecs
    GET #1, , comic    ' Read the next record
    LPRINT "Title: "; comic.title
    LPRINT "Date: "; comic.comDate; TAB(20); "Price: ";
    LPRINT USING "#.##"; comic.price
    LPRINT "Condition: "; comic.condition
    LPRINT
NEXT recs
CLOSE #1
END
```

YIKES!

You'll notice a strange-looking statement before the LPRINT section's FOR loop. The LOF() function returns the total number of bytes in the file. If you divide that number by the record length of the record variable, you'll get the number of records in the file.

Things You Can Do

After you understand reading and writing random-access files, you can write more powerful applications. Often, the user wants to change data stored in a random-access file. The change is easy if the user knows the record number. You might do something like this:

```
INPUT "What is the record number you want to change"; rec
GET #1, rec, comic
' Code to display the data currently in the record
' Let user input new data for the record
PUT #1, rec, comic    ' Write back the new data
```

Of course, how often will the user know the record number of the data to change? Probably rarely or never. Therefore, you have to get more sophisticated. You might have to ask the user for a title (or if this were a business inventory system, you would ask for a part number; or if this were an employee system, you would ask for a Social Security number). Then you could search the file for a title with the code outlined next:

```
DIM ti AS STRING * 15
INPUT "What is the title of the comic you want to change"; ti
' Read through the file looking for the user's title
FOR rec = 1 TO numRecs
   GET #1, rec, comic    ' Read the next record
```

```
        IF (comic.title = ti) THEN
            ' Prompt user for new data for this comic
            PUT #1, rec, comic
            EXIT FOR    ' Don't read rest of file
        END IF
    NEXT rec
```

Well, this chapter certainly gave you food for thought!
You can now write programs that store data in files,
then go back into those files as the data changes and
update the files.

Happy Hunting

 Store data in random-access files if specific data values in the
file are subject to change.

 Tell QBasic what your file's record looks like with TYPE.

 Define your record variables with the extended format of DIM
after you've created the record format with TYPE.

 Use GET # and PUT # to read and write data at any location in
a random-access file.

Charged

 Don't use data type suffixes on your TYPE field names. The AS
clause inside TYPE declares the data type.

 Don't read past the end of a file. Use LOF() as described in
this chapter so that you'll know when your program reads
the last line in a random-access file.

In Review

The goal of this chapter is to extend your knowledge of disk files by showing you how to create, read, and change random-access files. Working with random-access files is some of the most advanced work you can do with QBasic. Unlike with sequential files, you can change data within a random-access file without having to rewrite the entire file.

Reading and writing to random-access files requires that you create records with the TYPE command. The GET and PUT statements then read and write that record data to the random-access disk file that you've opened.

Code Example

```
' TV station tracking program
TYPE myTVrec
  channel   AS INTEGER
  station   AS STRING *20
END TYPE
DIM tvVar AS myTVrec    ' Create a record variable
OPEN "c:\tv.dat" FOR RANDOM AS #1 LEN = LEN(tvVar)
FOR i = 1 to 3
   INPUT "What is your favorite channel"; tvVar.channel
   INPUT "What is the name of the station"; tvVar.station
   PUT #1, , tvVar
NEXT i
' Now read the file backward
PRINT "Here is your list of favorite stations:"
GET #1, 3, tvVar
PRINT "Station: "; tvVar.station; " Channel:"; tvVar.channel
GET #1, 2, tvVar    ' Read second favorite
PRINT "Station: "; tvVar.station; " Channel:"; tvVar.channel
GET #1, 1, tvVar    ' Read top favorite
PRINT "Station: "; tvVar.station; " Channel:"; tvVar.channel
CLOSE #1
END
```

Code Analysis

This program creates a new record named `myTVrec` that contains an integer and a string. A variable is reserved for that record by using a `DIM` statement. (`DIM` reserves arrays, matrices, and record variables.)

A random-access file is then opened, and the user is asked for his or her favorite stations and channels. The data is written to a random-access file and then read back into the program backward before closing the file. There is no way to read a sequential file backward.

Part VI
Detour with Subroutines

"That's the last time I take a detour through Lake Victoria!"

22

What About Long Programs?

Organize Them with GOSUB

This chapter begins a new direction in your QBasic programming. You now know all the fundamentals of the language. Although there are several commands this book has not covered, most of them are just extensions of the commands you now know. It is time to turn your attention to the future.

Most of your QBasic programs will be longer than the short ones you see here or in any other book on QBasic. Most "real-world" programs are several pages long. As your needs grow, so will your QBasic program size. Before you get too deep, this section of the book will explain how you can better organize your code to make it easier to write and maintain.

GOSUB-RETURN

You'll never see a GOSUB without a RETURN somewhere else in the program. A GOSUB is a little like a detour—GOSUB overrides the normal flow of a program. Instead of the statement *after* the GOSUB executing, a completely different part of the program executes. Eventually, a RETURN statement returns the execution to where the GOSUB began, and the program continues sequentially from there.

PSST! The section of code executed by the GOSUB statement is called a *subroutine.* A subroutine is a small section within a larger program that executes when you *call* the subroutine with a GOSUB statement.

HMM... Figure 22.1 gives you an overview of the GOSUB's purpose. A RETURN statement always ends a subroutine's code so that QBasic knows when to get back on the path it was on before GOSUB changed the course.

Figure 22.1.

GOSUB causes a program to jump to another location for a while before returning.

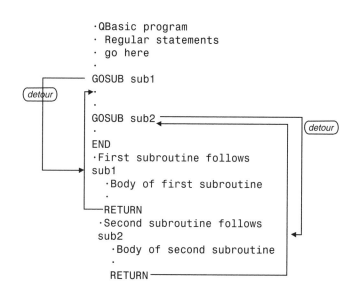

Statement Labels

Figure 22.1 hints at one more item you need to understand before mastering subroutines and GOSUB. QBasic has to know exactly where the statements are that you want GOSUB to execute. Therefore, you have to label the first statement in the subroutine with a *label* (good name, huh?). A label is a one-word description, from 1 to 40 characters long, that ends with a colon (:). All of these are valid labels:

```
Here:    PayCalc:    sub1:    PrintRoutine:
```

Here is the format of GOSUB:

```
GOSUB label
```

YIKES!

Never follow the label with a colon in a GOSUB statement. The colon goes *only* after the label at the start of the subroutine.

Suppose a subroutine printed your name and address and you wanted to execute that subroutine from various places in a program. Here is an outline of such a program with the full subroutine's code specified:

```
' Outline of a program that calls
' a name and address subroutine
GOSUB nameAddr       ' Calls the subroutine
'
' More statements go here
'
GOSUB nameAddr        ' Calls the subroutine
'
' More statements go here
'
GOSUB nameAddr        ' Calls the subroutine
'
END     ' END keeps QBasic from executing into the subroutine
nameAddr:             ' Label that begins the subroutine
   PRINT "Kay Bryson"
   PRINT "1013 S. Illinois"
   PRINT "Muskogee, OK  74003"
   RETURN
```

Notice that the body of the subroutine is indented. The indention helps you distinguish the subroutine from the rest of the program.

The preceding program shows an outline that executes the primary body of the program (the code that would go before the subroutine). The subroutine code labeled nameAddr: is called to execute three times because there are three GOSUBs in the program. The END statement keeps the program execution from "falling through" to the subroutine. Without END, QBasic would "fall through" and execute the PRINT statements one last time, then would issue an error when the RETURN is reached without a corresponding GOSUB to get there.

Why Do I Need Subroutines?

If you are asking why you need subroutines, you are right on track. The need for subroutines will become more obvious the more you program and the longer your programs get. As you write long programs, you will find yourself needing to execute the same set of statements several times within a single program. Instead of typing a copy of the code in more than one place, you can stick the code at the bottom of your program, in a subroutine with a label and RETURN statement, and then call that code with a GOSUB statement when you want the subroutine executed.

Not only is your code smaller when you use subroutines (because you don't have to repeat the same lines), but the program is easier to follow later if you need to change or modify it.

Any time your program performs one specific task, such as printing a check or calculating a person's payroll figure, consider putting that code in a subroutine. By using subroutines, you *modularize* your code. The modules, or subroutines, are pieces of the program that are controlled by the GOSUBs above them. If you want to rearrange the program's execution order, you will not have to rearrange code but will only need to rearrange GOSUBs, which are easier to manage.

GOSUB subroutine calls are nice to use in SELECT CASE statements. Instead of making the SELECT CASE contain lots of code, you can keep the SELECT CASE short by calling subroutines.

Here is a program that displays a menu that asks the user for a
certain conversion. A subroutine call performs the conversion
desired.

```
' Converts feet to/from meters without subroutines
' There are 39.37 inches in a meter, so there
' are 3.28 feet in a meter
CLS
PRINT "** Conversion **"
DO
   PRINT
   PRINT "Do you want to"
   PRINT "1. Convert meters to feet"
   PRINT "2. Convert feet to meters"
   PRINT "3. Exit the program"
   INPUT "What is your choice"; ch
   PRINT
   SELECT CASE ch
      CASE 1
         GOSUB MetToFeet    ' Call a subroutine
      CASE 2
         GOSUB FeetToMet    ' Call a subroutine
   END SELECT
LOOP UNTIL (ch = 3)
END
' Subroutines follow
MetToFeet:
   INPUT "What is the meter value you want converted"; meter
   feet = meter * 3.28
   PRINT "The number of feet in"; meter; "meters is"; feet
   RETURN
FeetToMet:
   INPUT "What is the feet value you want converted"; feet
   meter = feet / 3.28
   PRINT "The number of meters in"; feet; "feet is"; meter
   RETURN
```

PSST! If you want to put END after the last subroutine in a program,
you can, but QBasic does not require it.

Happy Hunting

 Use GOSUB to call a subroutine and RETURN to make sure that QBasic goes back properly when the subroutine is finished.

 Put END before the first subroutine's code so that QBasic does not fall through and execute the first subroutine.

 Use subroutine calls to keep SELECT CASE statements cleaner.

Charged

 Don't repeat sections of code throughout a program. Put the code in a subroutine and use GOSUB to go to the code.

 Don't use a colon after a label in a GOSUB statement. The colon follows labels only at the *start* of the subroutine, not at the subroutine call.

In Review

The goal of this chapter is to show you how to break long programs into more manageable sections called subroutines. The GOSUB statements let one part of a program trigger the execution of another part before the first one resumes. Grouping similar statements into their own separate part of the program makes your programs easier to write and test.

Code Example

```
' This is a subroutine that beeps and
' gives the user a warning. This subroutine
' could be called with GOSUB before the
' rest of the program prints on the printer.
```

```
prWarn:
   BEEP
   PRINT "Be sure to turn on your printer"
   PRINT "and make sure that it has plenty"
   PRINT "of paper."
   PRINT
   INPUT "Press Enter to continue...", en$
   RETURN
```

Code Analysis

This code shows a subroutine that could be called before the rest of the program prints to the printer (with LPRINT). LPRINT cannot write to a printer that has no paper or that is not turned on. Instead of the rest of the program warning the user before each LPRINT, the rest of the program only has to call the subroutine like this:

```
GOSUB prWarn
```

Can I Write My Own Functions?

No Problem with User-Defined Functions

Remember all those built-in functions that save you so much time? The functions such as LEFT$(), INT(), and the rest are nice because you don't have to write the code needed to do those jobs. As a matter of fact, the only problem with the built-in functions is that there aren't enough of them. It would be great if you could write your own function and then use that function throughout a program just as if that function were built in.

You *can* write your own functions! These are called *user-defined functions*. You can write string functions or numeric functions. Remember that a function always returns a value. For instance, MID$() returns a substring within another string. Also, you pass built-in functions arguments. If you pass INT() the argument 13.4, INT() returns 13 (the integer portion of 13.4).

The functions that you write will receive arguments and return values. Functions are a lot like subroutines. If it weren't for the arguments and return values, a function would be a subroutine.

PSST!   The functions that you write can return only single values, just as the built-in functions do.

Skip This, It's Technical

The concept of a programming language function comes from mathematics. In math, the term $f(x)$ is a function that receives an argument x and always returns a value based on x. That's just what QBasic functions do! As with math functions, you can write QBasic functions that receive more than one argument, but no matter how many arguments you pass, a function can return only one value at a time.

DEF FN() Does the Trick!

QBasic's DEF FN() statement enables you to define your own functions. After you define a function, the rest of the program can then use that function as if it were a function supplied with the language. Here is the format of DEF FN():

```
DEF FNname (arguments)
    Block of QBasic statements
    FNname = expression
END DEF
```

> **HMM...** The data type suffix at the end of the function's name is important. If the function is to return a string, be sure that the function name ends with a $. If the function returns a double-precision value, end the function's name with a #, and so on.

Remember that the RND function returns a random number from 0 to 1. Also, before calling RND (the only numeric function that does not require an argument or parentheses), you need to call RANDOMIZE TIMER to truly randomize the RND call (I know, it seems silly, but QBasic requires it). Rarely will your programs need a random number from 0 to 1. More likely, you'll need a random number from 1 to another value such as 6 (to simulate a dice roll). You can write your own function that calls RANDOMIZE TIMER for you and takes two arguments: the low number and high number of the range of random numbers needed. Here is such a function to clarify things a bit:

```
DEF FNrndRnge (low, high)
    RANDOMIZE TIMER
    rNum = INT(RND * (high - low + 1)) + low
    FNrndRnge = rNum
END DEF
```

YIKES!

You can probably follow everything in this function until you get to the fourth line. The name of the function, FNrndRnge, is being assigned a value! This is the method you use to specify the return value. In other words, the return value of the user-defined function FNrndRnge is rNum.

The low and high values are the arguments. In other words, when the program calls this function, two arguments must be specified that indicate the low and high values in the range of random numbers needed. Here is one way you might call this function from somewhere else in the program:

```
rouletteSpin = FNrndRnge(1, 36)
```

The variable rouletteSpin will be assigned the return value of the FNrndRnge function. Because a roulette wheel spin can produce a number from 1 to 36 (ruling out 0 and 00—we're using the European roulette rules here), the function call shown requests a random number from 1 to 36. The function then randomizes the random-number generator via the RANDOMIZE statement and then uses the two arguments to convert the random number from 0 to 1 into a number within the range of the low to high variables (which hold 1 and 36 respectively given the function call shown previously).

Here is a small program that produces some roulette wheel spins:

```
' Program to demonstrate some roulette spins
DEF FNrndRnge (low, high)
   RANDOMIZE TIMER
   rNum = INT(RND * (high - low + 1)) + low
   FNrndRnge = rNum
END DEF
' Actual program begins here
CLS
PRINT "Welcome to the study of roulette!"
PRINT
```

```
PRINT "Here are 30 random spins of a roulette wheel:"
FOR cnt = 1 TO 30
   PRINT FNrndRnge(1, 36);
NEXT cnt
PRINT
PRINT "Would you have bet properly?"
END
```

A String Function Example

Have you heard of the term *palindrome*? A palindrome is a word or phrase spelled the same forward and backward. Here are a couple of the more popular ones:

```
Race car
```

```
Draw pupil's lip upward!
```

There are several ways to write programs that test for palindromes. One approach is to convert a string to a uniform case (QBasic's built-in UCASE$() function handles that) and then strip the string of its special characters and spaces (you look at only alphabetic characters when testing for palindromes). Using this method would leave compressed phrases like these:

```
RACECAR
```

```
DRAWPUPILSLIPUPWARD
```

The last step is to reverse the phrase into another string variable and test to see whether the reversed string is equal to the forward string.

Two user-defined string functions will handle the busy work of palindrome testing. Here is a string function that returns an upper-case stripped version of its argument:

```
DEF FNstrip$ (pal$)
   stripStrn$ = ""    ' Start with an empty string
   upPal$ = UCASE$(pal$)
```

```
    FOR i = 1 TO LEN(pal$)
       IF (MID$(upPal$, i, 1) >= "A") AND
       ➡(MID$(upPal$, i, 1) <= "Z") THEN
             stripStrn$ = stripStrn$ + MID$(upPal$, i, 1)
       END IF
    NEXT i
    FNstrip$ = stripStrn$      ' Return the newly built string
END DEF
```

YIKES!

You've never seen a plus sign applied to a string before. The + tacks characters onto the end of a string. FNstrip$( ) adds a character to the new string from the argument if that character is an uppercase letter.

Here is a function that returns the reverse of whatever string is passed to it:

```
DEF FNrev$ (pal$)
   revStr$ = ""      ' Start with a blank string
   FOR i = LEN(pal$) TO 1 STEP -1
                              ' Step back through the string
      revStr$ = revStr$ + MID$(pal$, i, 1)
   NEXT i
   FNrev$ = revStr$
END DEF
```

After you've entered these two functions, it is very easy to test for palindromes. The following code could appear after the preceding function definitions in a program to tell the user whether the entered word or phrase is a palindrome:

```
CLS
INPUT "Please enter a word or phrase...", userPal$
stripped$ = FNstrip$(userPal$)  ' Strip the user's string
revUserSt$ = FNrev$(stripped$)  ' Reverse the stripped string
IF (stripped$ = revUserSt$) THEN
   PRINT "You entered a palindrome!"
ELSE
```

```
    PRINT "You did not type a palindrome."
END IF
END
```

Happy Hunting

 Write a user-defined function if you want to simulate a built-in function call.

 Use the DEF FN statement to define your own functions.

 Put the data type suffix of the function's return value after the function name that you define.

Charged

 Don't forget to assign the return value to the function's name inside the user-defined function.

In Review

The goal of this chapter is to show you how to write your own functions that supplement QBasic's built-in functions. Use the DEF FN statement to write your functions, and then you can call by name the function that you write.

Functions differ from subroutines because functions always return values. A function can return a single value, and you can then use that return value, either a string or a number, in a QBasic statement or expression.

Code Example

```
DEF FNareaCir(rad)
    pi = 3.14159
    FNareaCir = pi * rad ^ 2
END DEF
```

Code Analysis

This user-defined function takes one argument, a circle's radius, and computes and returns the area of the circle. The rest of the program could find the area of any circle by calling this function and passing it a radius value such as this line does:

```
PRINT FNareaCir(5)
```

Can I Separate My Subroutines Further?

Use Subroutine Procedures

If subroutines and user-defined functions are good (and they are), *subroutine procedures* are really good! Subroutine procedures were not available with versions of BASIC prior to QBasic. Bringing subroutine procedures into the language makes QBasic able to compete with the "big guys," such as Pascal, C, and FORTRAN.

A subroutine procedure is a subroutine that is completely separated from the rest of the program. A QBasic program that contains one or more subroutine procedures is stored in one program file on the disk when you save it with **File Save**. However, as long as the program is loaded in the QBasic editor, you'll work with the program in pieces, never being able to see the subroutine procedure at the same time as you see any of the rest of the program.

HMM... When you added subroutines to your programs in Chapter 22, "What About Long Programs?" the subroutines went at the bottom of the program, and you could see both the program and the subroutines on-screen at the same time. Now, you won't be able to see them at the same time because QBasic wants you to think of subroutine procedures as though they are a completely different section of the program.

YIKES!

A subroutine procedure is really just a subroutine, but it is a subroutine that is designated by a special SUB keyword and that is edited in a different section of QBasic from the rest of the program.

Specifying Subroutine Procedures

The primary difference between a subroutine and a subroutine procedure is that a subroutine is called with GOSUB and has a label at the beginning and RETURN at the end. A subroutine procedure is called by the CALL statement, begins with SUB, and ends with an END SUB statement. Here is the format of a subroutine procedure:

```
SUB procedureName
    One or more QBasic statements
END SUB
```

Here is the format of CALL:

```
CALL procedureName
```

  CALL is to a subroutine procedure what GOSUB is to a subroutine.

Subroutine procedures never contain RETURN statements. When the subroutine procedure ends, QBasic knows to return the program control to the calling portion of the program.

Learn It by Trying It

There is no way to describe QBasic procedures adequately without walking you through a short example. You have to see for yourself what QBasic does when you begin writing code for a subroutine procedure. As you read this section, keep this in mind: A subroutine procedure is *just* a subroutine. However, unlike with the subroutines you read about in Chapter 22, QBasic completely separates subroutine procedures from the rest of your program.

At the end of the preceding chapter, you saw how to write a palindrome program using user-defined functions. The user-defined string functions shown in that program are fine, but those same routines make good subroutine procedure candidates as well. Therefore, this chapter shows you the same program modified so that its palindrome checking is done inside subroutine procedures.

The following section of a program contains two calls to subroutine procedures. Type this program into QBasic.

```
' Program with two subroutine procedures
CLS
INPUT "Please enter a word or phrase...", userPal$

' The subroutine procedure calls follow
CALL stripIt(userPal$)
                      ' Strip the string of special characters
stripped$ = userPal$      ' Save before reversing the string
CALL reverseIt(userPal$)  ' Reverse the contents of the string

' If the pre-reversed string is equal to the reversed string,
' a palindrome was typed
IF (stripped$ = userPal$) THEN    ' If
   PRINT "You entered a palindrome!"
ELSE
   PRINT "You did not type a palindrome."
END IF
END
```

You now must include the code that does the work of stripping and reversing the string. We'll do that in two separate subroutine procedures. To see how QBasic handles subroutine procedures, move the cursor to a line or two below the END statement, and type this first line of the first subroutine procedure:

```
SUB stripIt(userPal$)
```

YIKES!

Did you see what QBasic did? Figure 24.1 shows your screen at this point. QBasic got rid of all the code except for the SUB statement. Then QBasic added an END SUB at the end of the subroutine procedure (because all subroutine procedures need an END SUB, and QBasic knows it). QBasic is now waiting for you to fill in the body of the subroutine procedure.

Figure 24.1.

QBasic takes control of the situation when you type a SUB statement.

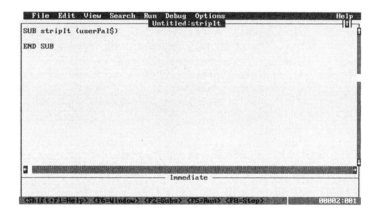

The variable userPal$ is the subroutine procedure's argument. As with functions, you can pass one or more arguments to a QBasic subroutine procedure. The procedure can then change those arguments.

Skip This, It's Technical

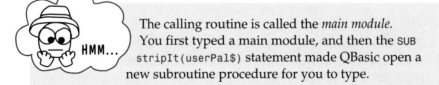

QBasic hides all data values inside a subroutine procedure from the calling code. If you want a value in the calling code to be worked on by a subroutine procedure, you must pass that value inside the parentheses as shown in this example, and the SUB statement must list the argument as done here as well.

Insert the following code between the SUB and the END SUB statements. The code is just like the FNstrip$ function code you saw near the end of the preceding chapter, except that the passed string is modified so that the calling code can work with the modified string.

```
stripStrn$ = ""              ' Start with an empty string
upPal$ = UCASE$(userPal$)    ' Convert passed string to upper
FOR i = 1 TO LEN(userPal$)
   IF (MID$(upPal$, i, 1) >= "A") AND
   ➥(MID$(upPal$, i, 1) <= "Z") THEN
      stripStrn$ = stripStrn$ + MID$(upPal$, i, 1)
   END IF
NEXT i
userPal$ = stripStrn$     ' Change the argument so the calling
           ' code's userPal$ is now stripped of special characters
```

The calling routine is called the *main module.* You first typed a main module, and then the SUB stripIt(userPal$) statement made QBasic open a new subroutine procedure for you to type.

It is now time to type the second subroutine procedure. Place the cursor below the END SUB statement and type this:

```
SUB reverseIt(userPal$)
```

As it always does, QBasic opens up a new editing window for the reverseIt() subroutine procedure and enables you to enter that procedure's code. Type the following code between the SUB and the END SUB statements:

```
revStr$ = ""     ' Start with a blank string
FOR i = LEN(userPal$) TO 1 STEP -1
                         ' Step back through the string
   revStr$ = revStr$ + MID$(userPal$, i, 1)
NEXT i
userPal$ = revStr$    ' Reverse the string so the main
              ' module can work with the reversed string
```

You are now done with one complete program that contains two subroutine procedures. Run the program a few times to see how the subroutine procedures perform the palindrome test. Use these palindromes to test the program:

```
Faced decaf
```

```
Fled a mad elf
```

YIKES!

If you save the program, QBasic adds the following statements to the top of the main module whether or not you want it to:

```
DECLARE SUB stripIt(userPal$)
DECLARE SUB reverseIt(userPal$)
```

QBasic wants these lines (you could have typed them yourself, but why do so when QBasic will do it for you?) at the top of any program with subroutine procedures.

When you save the program or print a listing with **File Print**, QBasic saves and displays the entire program with subroutine procedures and all. In the QBasic editing window, however, QBasic ensures that you can work with only one procedure or the main module at a time.

Getting Around

You might want to move back and forth between subroutine procedures and the main module as you write programs that use subroutine procedures. The F2 key is the shortcut key to jump back and forth between subroutine procedures and the main module. Press F2 now and you'll see a list of three items: the main module, the reverseIt subroutine procedure, and the stripIt subroutine procedure.

You can press the arrow keys and press Enter or else click with the mouse to choose which one of the three procedures you want to edit next. Therefore, if you are in the reverseIt subroutine procedure and want to edit code in the stripIt procedure, press F2 and select the stripIt procedure.

Happy Hunting

 Use subroutine procedures to really separate subroutines from the main module that called them.

 Pass the variables you need to share among subroutine procedures inside parentheses just as you do with function arguments that you pass.

 Press F2 to jump from subroutine procedure to subroutine procedure.

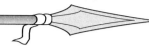

Charged

 Don't call subroutine procedures with GOSUB—use CALL instead.

 Don't place a RETURN at the end of a subroutine procedure. END SUB is all you need.

In Review

The goal of this chapter is to show you how to make subroutines even more powerful by putting them into subroutine procedures. Subroutine procedures are physically separated from your programs. QBasic separates the variables used in the procedures, so you must pass the variables to the subroutine procedures, whereas you don't have to pass variables to GOSUB subroutines.

Code Example

```
DECLARE SUB encode (wrd$)
' Ask the user for a word to encode
INPUT "What word do you want to encode"; wrd$
CALL encode(wrd$)
END

SUB encode (wrd$)
    s$ = ""
    FOR i = 1 TO LEN(wrd$)
        s$ = s$ + CHR$(ASC(MID$(wrd$, i, 1)) + 1)
    NEXT i
    PRINT s$
END SUB
```

Code Analysis

This program contains a subroutine procedure that receives a string variable and encodes the string by adding 1 to the ASCII value of each letter. The subroutine procedure then converts that ASCII value back to a character and stores the character in a new string named s$.

Run this program and look at the encoded value for *HAL.*

Part VII
Playing Around

"Good shot, old boy! You've really improved your swing!"

Will QBasic Produce Sounds?

Make Noise with QBasic

Let the fun begin! QBasic programming is not all work—you can have fun as well. This chapter takes up where BEEP left off. Rather than a single tone, you can play any noise or song through your PC's speaker with the help of QBasic. The SOUND command enables you to control the length, number, and tone of notes.

YIKES!

Programming sound with the SOUND command is fun, but your PC is capable of producing only one note at a time. Unless you have an add-on sound card and understand the software that goes with it, programming noise is limited, but it beats not being able to produce sound at all.

Listening to SOUND

Without further ado, type in this program and sit back and listen when you run it:

```
' Program that produces nonsense noises
FOR i = 1 TO 3
  SOUND 440, 3
  SOUND 450, 3
  SOUND 460, 3
NEXT
FOR i = 1 TO 3
  SOUND 840, 3
  SOUND 850, 3
  SOUND 860, 3
NEXT i
FOR i = 1 TO 2
  SOUND 440, 3
  SOUND 450, 3
  SOUND 460, 3
NEXT
SOUND 440, 6
SOUND 490, 6
```

```
SOUND 550, 6
SOUND 590, 6
END
```

YIKES!

OK, the author is an *author*, not a *composer*!

Looking at SOUND

The SOUND command produces sound through your PC's speaker. Here is the format of SOUND:

SOUND *frequency, duration*

The *frequency* determines which note is sounded. The *frequency* value is a number from 32 to 32767. The higher the *frequency*, the faster the note vibrates and the higher the note sounds.

PSST! Humans can rarely hear notes higher than *frequency* values of 20000.

The *duration* determines how long the note sounds. It takes a *duration* of 18.2 to sound a note for a single second. To sound a note for two seconds, you would specify 36.4 as the duration, and so on.

Getting the exact *frequency* of a number is not always easy. You often have to take a guess and then listen to see whether your guess sounds correct. Microsoft, the maker of QBasic, does tell us that a *frequency* of 440 produces the same note as the A below middle C on a piano. If you double that *frequency* to 880, you'll hear the A above middle C. Continuing to double 440 gets you each octave

above, and continuing to halve 440 gets you each octave below the
A below middle C.

YIKES!

If you are unfamiliar with music or pianos, don't fret. This
discussion is useful to those who need help mapping
some frequencies onto specific notes.

Figure 25.1 shows a portion of a piano keyboard and some frequencies you can use for the A's. You'll have to do your own
extrapolation to get the frequencies of the other notes. Most QBasic
programmers use SOUND to produce special effects instead of for
playing tunes.

Figure 25.1.

*Mapping some
frequency values
onto a piano
keyboard.*

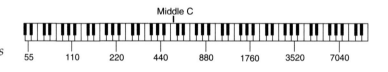

The following program plays each of the A's shown in the figure for
one second.

```
' Sounds out each octave's A for one second each
SOUND 55, 18.2
SOUND 110, 18.2
SOUND 220, 18.2
SOUND 440, 18.2
SOUND 880, 18.2
SOUND 1760, 18.2
SOUND 3520, 18.2
SOUND 7040, 18.2
END
```

To give you an idea of the range of sounds possible, here is a
program that sounds each frequency for a small duration and
then runs back down the chromatic scale:

```
' Produces all sounds from low to high and low again
CLS
PRINT "Going up, please!"
' Play the notes going up the frequency scale
FOR freq = 37 TO 20000 STEP 10
    SOUND freq, .25
NEXT freq
' Play the notes going down the frequency scale
PRINT "DOWN, DOwn, down, ..."
FOR freq = 20000 TO 37 STEP -10
    SOUND freq, .25
NEXT freq
END
```

A STEP value of 10 was used in the program because it takes so long to cycle through every possible frequency.

The next program gives you some more ideas about the special-effect sounds that are possible. Run the program and you'll hear something that sounds like a clash between a space computer battle and a bad dream!

```
COLOR 12, 2
CLS
LOCATE 12, 34
PRINT "Ooohh..."
' Weird effects
FOR i = 1 TO 35
    freq = INT(RND * 2700) + 500
    dur = INT(RND * 3) + 1
    SOUND freq, dur
NEXT i

' Settling down a little!
FOR freq = 750 TO 450 STEP -7
    SOUND freq, 1
    SOUND 800 - freq, 1
NEXT freq
END
```

PSST!   If you don't have a color monitor, get rid of the COLOR statement.

Happy Hunting

 Add noise with SOUND to really get your user's attention!

 Before writing a song with SOUND, you need to practice with SOUND until you find the frequencies that match the notes you need.

Charged

 Don't attempt to SOUND a frequency lower than 37 or higher than 32767.

In Review

The goal of this chapter is to teach you about the SOUND statement and how you can use SOUND to add sounds and music to your programs. SOUND requires two arguments, a frequency and the duration (in ticks per second).

Code Example

```
SOUND 1000, 4.5
GOSUB pause
SOUND 800, 2
GOSUB pause
SOUND 800, 1.5
```

```
GOSUB pause
SOUND 900, 3
GOSUB pause
SOUND 800, 6
GOSUB pause
SOUND 985, 2.5
GOSUB pause
SOUND 1060, 6
END
pause:
   SOUND 24000, 4    ' Cannot hear this!
   RETURN
```

Code Analysis

This program sounds a series of notes that produce the "Shave and a haircut—two bits!" theme. The subroutine seems to produce a staccato-like pause between sounds, but the pause is actually a note playing at frequency 24000, which is too high for the human ear to hear.

When Can I Draw?

Now, with QBasic Graphics

While adding sound to your programs, you might as well add some fancy graphics as well! This chapter explores ways that you can draw on the screen. You must have a VGA color monitor and graphics card to make the programs in this chapter and the next chapter work.

 If you are unsure which graphics adapter and monitor you have, don't worry! Try one of the programs here. If you see graphics, you have a monitor that is compatible. If not, you will not have harmed anything by trying.

Setting the Screen with SCREEN

Before displaying anything other than text, you must change the mode of your screen with the SCREEN command. Here is the format of SCREEN:

SCREEN *mode*

The mode can be any of the *mode* values shown in the tear-out card of this book.

The SCREEN *mode* values indicate the kind of graphics that you can draw. When in graphics mode—as opposed to text mode, the default (SCREEN *mode* 0)—you can draw so many lines and columns of graphics dots. Each dot is called a *pixel* (which means *picture element*). A pixel is the row and column intersection. For SCREEN *mode* 1, for example, you can turn on up to 200 rows and 320 columns of graphics pixels.

The more rows and columns a SCREEN *mode* provides, the better looking your graphics will be. The pixels will be closer together and will provide straighter lines and curvier circles.

Although we'll save learning about colors until the next chapter, you'll notice that some SCREEN *mode* values enable you to have more colors at one time than others.

PSST! You don't have to issue a CLS command to clear your graphics screens. Each SCREEN statement erases the screen and sets up the screen for the resulting graphics mode needed.

Connect the Dots

The most fundamental graphics command you can specify is turning on and off a pixel. The PSET command turns on a pixel, and the PRESET command turns off a pixel. Here are the formats of the PSET and PRESET commands:

```
PSET [STEP] (col, row)
```

and

```
PRESET [STEP] (col, row)
```

The minimum *col* and *row* values you can specify are both 0. The maximum *row* and *col* values are determined by the SCREEN *mode* you have set. For example, if you have specified SCREEN 12, the maximum *row* value is 479 (there are 480 total rows, and the first one begins at 0), and the maximum *col* value is 639.

To set the screen in a graphics mode and turn on three dots, you can do this:

Fun Fact
The first graphics-oriented commercial video game was called PONG. PONG, a simple (by today's standards) video tennis game, started the video arcade craze that began in the late 1970s.

```
SCREEN 12           ' You must have VGA for this
PSET (100, 100)     ' 101st column and the 101st row
PSET (25, 210)      ' 26th column and the 211th row
PSET (201, 315)     ' 202nd column and the 316th row
```

YIKES!

If you run this short program, you'll have to look closely to see the three dots. SCREEN *mode* 12 is a high *resolution* (a fancy name for the density of graphics rows and columns), and the three pixels are small.

You can print text while displaying a graphics screen using PRINT, just as you do on a text screen.

The STEP option of the PSET command (and its mirror-image PRESET command) lightens your work a little if you have to draw several pixels close together. STEP indicates a *relative placement* of the new dots on-screen compared to the dots you previously drew with PSET. For example, to draw a straight line of four pixels, you can do this:

```
SCREEN 12           ' You must have VGA for this
PSET (100, 100)
PSET (100, 101)
PSET (100, 102)
PSET (100, 103)
```

You can also use STEP in the last three commands. The *row* and *col* values of STEP indicate how far away from the preceding PSET you want dots drawn.

```
SCREEN 12           ' You must have VGA for this
PSET (100, 100)
PSET STEP(0, 1)
PSET STEP(0, 1)
PSET STEP(0, 1)
```

PRESET does the opposite of PSET. PRESET turns off a pixel at the specified *row* and *col* value. The following statements turn off the four pixels just drawn. Notice that last statement uses STEP for relative placement of the last turned-off pixel.

```
PRESET (100, 100)
PRESET (100, 101)
PRESET (100, 102)
PRESET STEP(0, 1)
```

Draw Lines with LINE

You can draw lines with PSET, but it takes a lot of typing and is slow. The QBasic LINE command draws lines quickly and easily. Here is the format of LINE:

```
LINE [STEP] (col, row) - [STEP] (col, row)
```

A line is determined by two end points. Therefore, LINE requires that you specify two column and row intersection pairs (the PSET requires only one pair). QBasic then draws a line between those points. The following LINE statement draws a line from the upper-left screen pixel to the lower-right screen pixel:

```
LINE (0, 0)-(639, 479)   ' Draws a diagonal line
```

PSST! As with PSET, you can use STEP on subsequent LINE commands to draw another line starting next to the place where the preceding line left off.

Box It In!

It's easy to turn the LINE line-drawing command into a box-drawing command. Add , , B to any LINE command and QBasic draws a box. As with a line, a box can be drawn from only two row and column pairs (indicating the placement of the upper-left corner and the lower-right corner of the box).

Here is a statement that draws a box at the top of your screen (assuming that a SCREEN 12 statement has been issued):

```
LINE (50, 50)-(600, 225), , B
```

YIKES!

If you're wondering why the extra comma is needed, a color value will go there in the next chapter. For now, concentrate on the drawing of the box, and leave the blank between the two commas.

HMM...

You *could* draw a box with four LINE statements, but why bother when QBasic can draw the box for you?

Going Around in Circles

Without a circle, QBasic's drawing commands would stink! As always, QBasic comes to the rescue with a CIRCLE command. A circle is known by the location of its center point (an imaginary pixel in the center of the circle you want to draw) and its radius size in pixels. The radius of a circle is the length (in pixels) from its center point to an outer edge. A circle's diameter, or measurement from side to opposite side, is two times the radius value.

Here is the format of the CIRCLE command:

```
CIRCLE [STEP] (col, row), radius
```

The *col* and *row* values indicate where the center of the circle will be placed on the screen. The *radius* value indicates the number of pixels in the circle's radius. Here is a command that draws a circle in the center of the screen that has a radius of 50 pixels:

```
CIRCLE (320, 240), 50
```

The following program draws lots of circles on your computer's screen. The RND function makes sure that each circle's location and radius are different.

```
SCREEN 12
FOR cnt = 1 TO 50                    ' Draws 50 circles
   centerCol = INT(RND * 639) + 1  ' From 0 to 639
   centerRow = INT(RND * 479) + 1  ' From 0 to 479
   radius = INT(RND * 100) + 1       ' From 0 to 100
   CIRCLE (centerCol, centerRow), radius
NEXT cnt
END
```

Happy Hunting

 Play around with the graphics commands shown in this chapter. That's the only way you'll learn them. Many people feel that the graphics commands are difficult because they appear in the back of books (like this one) rather than up with the "easier" stuff. Not true! QBasic makes graphics easy.

 Use the PSET command to turn on individual pixels. Use PRESET to turn off individual pixels. LINE draws both lines and boxes, and CIRCLE draws circles.

Charged

 Don't attempt to specify a SCREEN *mode* value that your graphics adapter and monitor cannot support.

In Review

The goal of this chapter is to show you how to draw dots, lines, and circles on your screen. Graphics help produce user interest in your programs, and they certainly make your programs much more fun to use.

When you draw on-screen, you control a series of pixels (meaning picture elements) which are either on or off. The PSET and PRESET commands turn pixels on and off. The LINE command draws lines and boxes, and the CIRCLE command draws circles.

Code Example

```
SCREEN 12
LINE (1, 1)-(479, 639)
LINE (50, 50)-(200, 200), , B
CIRCLE (320, 240), 40
END
```

Code Analysis

These lines of code draw a line, a box, and a circle on-screen after first setting the video mode to a VGA graphics mode.

Is Black and White All I Get?

Add Pizzazz with Color

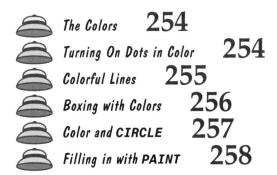

If you have a color monitor, there is no good reason to stick to black-and-white graphics! All the graphics commands you learned in the preceding chapter work in different colors. The SCREEN *mode* you specify determines how many colors the *mode* can handle. For instance, this book's tear-out card table of VGA SCREEN *mode* values explains that SCREEN *mode* 12 supports 16 different colors, and 13 supports up to 256.

PSST! This chapter is easy! You only have to add a color option to the graphics commands that you already know.

The Colors

This book's tear-out card contains a color table that you used for the text mode's COLOR command way back in Chapter 8, "How Do I Spruce Up My Output?" The colors in the table also work with most of the graphics commands.

PSST! Some graphics display adapters support more colors (in SCREEN *mode* 13) than the table describes. You'll have to experiment and learn some extended graphics commands (such as PALETTE, which is not covered here) if you want to access more than 16 colors at a time.

Turning On Dots in Color

The PSET command turns on white pixels unless you specify a different color (specified in the color value table). PRESET also

supports color values, but because PRESET is used to turn off pixels that are on, the color option isn't used with PRESET. To add color to a PSET pixel, follow PSET with a color value. The next statement turns on a red (color value 4) pixel at column 100, row 100:

```
PSET (100, 100), 4
```

The following program really makes the point! The program turns on pixels all over the screen in random colors. The RND function is used for both the color selection and the row and column positions.

```
SCREEN 12
RANDOMIZE TIMER
FOR dots = 1 TO 1500        ' 1500 dots all together
    colr = INT(RND * 16)    ' A color from 0 to 15
    row = INT(RND * 480)    ' A row from 0 to 479
    col = INT(RND * 640)    ' A column from 0 to 639
    PSET (col, row), colr   ' Turns on the pixel
NEXT dots
END
```

Color graphics aren't just for games. Many of today's business programs need color to emphasize a point or just to keep the user's attention. Viewing a colorful screen all day is much more appealing than looking at a drab *monochrome* (one-color) screen.

Colorful Lines

Add a color to the LINE command just as you did with PSET to draw colorful lines on-screen. Here is the format of LINE with the color option added:

```
LINE (col, row), color
```

The following LINE command draws a green line diagonally down the screen:

```
LINE (0, 0)-(639, 479), 2    ' Draws a green diagonal line
```

YIKES!

Be careful not to go outside your screen's boundaries. If you attempt to draw a line at column 1000 and row 1000, QBasic draws a line on the side of your monitor, and you'll have to use an eraser to get rid of it. (Just kidding! QBasic ignores your graphics-drawing request if you try to draw further than your screen row and column limits allow.)

Boxing with Colors

Drawing colorful boxes is just as easy as drawing colorful lines. Here is the format of the box-drawing LINE command with the color option:

```
LINE (col, row), color, B
```

The following program draws a bunch of boxes within boxes, each a different color. Figure 27.1 shows what the screen looks like. The FOR loop ensures that 15 boxes (one for every color except black) are drawn.

```
SCREEN 12
' Pretty box-drawings
begX = 0
begY = 0
endX = 639
endY = 479

FOR colr = 1 TO 15      ' Cycles through the colors
   LINE (begX, begY)-(endX, endY), colr, B
```

```
' Next, adjust the row and column pairs for the next box
begX = begX + 15
begY = begY + 15
endX = endX - 15
endY = endY - 15
NEXT colr
END
```

YIKES!

Resist the temptation to use color as the name of a variable. Remember that COLOR is a command name and you cannot assign names to variables that match the names of commands.

Figure 27.1.
Gosh, those colorful boxes are pretty!

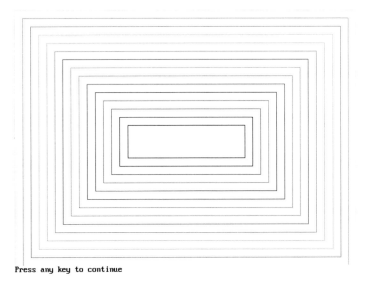

Press any key to continue

Color and CIRCLE

You guessed it...the COLOR statement also contains a color option. Here is the format of the CIRCLE command with a color value:

```
CIRCLE (col, row), radius, color
```

The following program draws a bunch of circles in random colors
all over the screen:

```
SCREEN 12
RANDOMIZE TIMER
FOR cnt = 1 TO 150                    ' Draws 150 circles
   centerCol = INT(RND * 639) + 1  ' From 0 to 639
   centerRow = INT(RND * 479) + 1  ' From 0 to 479
   colr = INT(RND * 16)               ' From 1 to 15
   radius = INT(RND * 100) + 1       ' From 0 to 100
   CIRCLE (centerCol, centerRow), radius, colr
NEXT cnt
END
```

PSST!   Run this program; its effect is interesting.

Filling In with PAINT

The PAINT command works just like a can of paint would work if
you poured the paint into a glass jar: The paint would fill every
nook and cranny of the jar, coloring the sides. After drawing a shape
on the screen, use PAINT to fill that shape with color, just as if you'd
poured paint into the shape. Here is the format of PAINT:

```
PAINT (col, row) [, [interiorColor], [borderColor]]
```

After you draw a shape on the screen, the PAINT's col and row
coordinates have to fall somewhere (anywhere) within that shape
for PAINT to color the entire area with the interiorColor value.
(If you don't specify an interior color, QBasic uses white.) The
borderColor tells PAINT where to stop painting. The borderColor
must be the same color as the outline of the shape being filled.

YIKES!

Paint only fully enclosed shapes. If a shape is not fully enclosed (such as a box with only three sides), the painted color overflows the shape and fills the rest of the screen (or until it runs up against the *borderColor* somewhere).

The slot machine game in Appendix B uses PAINT to fill in the interior colors for the spinning slot's pictures.

Happy Hunting

 Add a color value to any of the graphics commands to spice up your graphics.

Charged

Don't use the color option on PRESET unless you want to turn *on* a color with PRESET. Most QBasic programmers leave the color pixels to PSET and reserve PRESET for turning off pixels.

In Review

The goal of this chapter is to show you how to produce color graphics. Adding color to your graphics is extremely easy after you've mastered the graphics commands from the preceding chapter. Adding color requires no more than adding a numeric color value to the commands.

Code Example

```
SCREEN 12
FOR colr = 0 TO 15
   col = INT(RND * 279) + 1
   row = INT(RND * 439) + 1
   LINE (col, row)-(col + 200, row + 200), colr
NEXT colr
```

Code Analysis

This program produces lines randomly on-screen in each of the 16 colors.

Where Do I Go from Here?

This appendix lists some books that you might want to read now that you know QBasic. Some of the books are beginning-level books for other programming languages that you might be interested in learning. All are from Sams Publishing, and you can order them using the order form in the back of this book.

QBasic Programming 101

Readers take an active approach to learning QBasic in this step-by-step tutorial/workbook. Special features such as Find the Bug, Try

This, Think About, Finish the Program, and Still Confused? give the reader a thorough understanding of the language. This book discusses the PLAY and graphics features introduced in Chapter 11 of *Absolute Beginner's Guide to Programming.* (For beginning users.)

Teach Yourself QBasic in 21 Days

Users can achieve QBasic success now! Each lesson can be completed in two to three hours or less. Shaded syntax boxes, Q & A sections, and "Do's and Don'ts" sections reinforce the important topics within QBasic. (For beginning to intermediate users.)

Teach Yourself C in 21 Days

With this best-selling book, users can achieve C success now! Each lesson can be completed in two to three hours or less. Shaded syntax boxes, Q & A sections, and "Do's and Don'ts" sections reinforce the important topics within C. (For beginning to intermediate users.)

C++ Programming 101

Readers take an active approach to learning C++ in this step-by-step tutorial/workbook. Special features such as Find the Bug, Try This, Think About, Finish the Program, and Still Confused? give the reader a thorough understanding of the language. (For beginning users.)

Turbo C++ Programming 101

Readers take an active approach to learning Turbo C++ in this step-by-step tutorial/workbook. Special features such as Find the Bug, Try This, Think About, Finish the Program, and Still Confused? give the reader a thorough understanding of the language. (For beginning users.)

Turbo Pascal Programming 101

Readers take an active approach to learning Turbo Pascal in this step-by-step tutorial/workbook. Special features such as Find the Bug, Try This, Think About, Finish the Program, and Still Confused? give the reader a thorough understanding of the language. (For beginning users.)

B

Playing Around with a QBasic Slot Machine Game

Programming is not all work and no play—and the following slot machine game proves it! The game provides a long example that you can study as you master QBasic. The game is kept extremely simple; even so, a lot is happening in this program.

As with all well-written programs, this one is commented thoroughly. You will find more and more of the program understandable as you progress through the book.

PSST!   When you master enough of QBasic to understand the inner workings of the program, you'll want to explore graphics capabilities and add more symbols to the spinning wheels.

Numbers appear to the left of many code lines. These are the numbers of the chapters that discuss the concepts used in the line. If a line confuses you, refer to the appropriate chapter.

CH04
```
REM ***********************************************************
' Casino Slot Machine Game
' -----------------------
'
' This program lets you play a simplified computerized slot
' machine and keeps track of your winnings and your losses!
'
' Many of the concepts of this book are used in this game,
' including graphics and sound to add special effects.
'
' You must have a standard VGA adapter and monitor to run this
' game.
'
' The game was kept simple so as to demonstrate this book's
' concepts without adding too much complexity. As you get more
' comfortable with QBasic programming, you'll want to add more
' features!
'
' Suggested improvements to the game:
'
' 1. Adjust the randomness of the spin so that the lower-
'    paying combination (three bars) appears more often than
'    3 plums and cherries.
' 2. Add more symbols that don't pay but affect the odds even
'    further.
'
'
```

CH24
```
DECLARE SUB doWinSound ()
DECLARE SUB finalSpin (totalCash!)
DECLARE SUB spinReels ()
DECLARE SUB drawCherry (colPos%, rowPos%)
DECLARE SUB drawPlum (colPos%, rowPos%)
DECLARE SUB drawBar (colPos%, rowPos%)
```

```
CH22     GOSUB titleScreen     ' Print opening screen
         GOSUB getBetAmt        ' Get amount of money that user has
CH15     DO WHILE (totalCash > 0)
CH05       PRINT
CH08       PRINT USING "&$$###,.##"; "You have:"; totalCash; " to bet."
           PRINT "Press Enter to drop a quarter and pull the handle..."
CH07       INPUT "(Enter STOP to quit the game)"; ent$
CH12       IF (UCASE$(LEFT$(ent$, 1)) = "S") THEN
             EXIT DO
CH13       END IF
CH22       GOSUB setUpNewGame              ' Initialize totals and so forth
CH24       CALL spinReels           ' Go through a cycle of random spins
           CALL finalSpin(totalCash) ' Print last and fixed spin
                                      ' position and update total cash
                                      ' depending on result of the
                                      ' final spin.
CH15     LOOP
CH05     CLS
CH22     GOSUB finalMessage
         END


         '*********************************************************
         titleScreen:
CH04     ' This subroutine executes once for the program
CH26       SCREEN 9
CH08       COLOR 15, 1
CH05       PRINT "C a s i n o   A c t i o n ! ! !"
           PRINT "-----------------------------"
           PRINT
           PRINT "Welcome to the slot game of the century!"
           PRINT
           PRINT "This game lets you continue playing until you are"
           PRINT "ready to stop or until you run out of money."
           PRINT
           PRINT "Each spin costs you a quarter. Here are the payoffs:"
           PRINT
           PRINT "3 bars: 2.00"
CH24       CALL drawBar(140, 130)
           CALL drawBar(270, 130)
           CALL drawBar(400, 130)
CH05       PRINT
           PRINT
CH08       COLOR 15, 1
           PRINT "3 plums: 2.50"
           PRINT
           PRINT
```

```
CH24        CALL drawPlum(140, 170)
            CALL drawPlum(270, 170)
            CALL drawPlum(400, 170)
CH08        COLOR 15, 1
            PRINT "3 cherries: 3.00"
            PRINT
CH24        CALL drawCherry(140, 220)
            CALL drawCherry(270, 220)
            CALL drawCherry(400, 220)
CH22        RETURN


            '**************************************************************
            getBetAmt:
CH04        ' This subroutine gets the amount of the user's bet in
            ' quarters
CH05        PRINT "Remember, this is only a game. No wagering for real"
            PRINT "(unless you want a chance to win a LOT of CASHola!)"
            PRINT
CH07        INPUT "How many quarters do you have to bet"; quarters
CH06        totalCash = quarters * .25
CH22        RETURN


            '**************************************************************
            setUpNewGame:
CH11           RANDOMIZE TIMER
CH06           totalCash = totalCash - .25    ' Each spin costs a quarter
               numBars = 0
               numPlums = 0
               numCherries = 0
CH22           RETURN
            finalMessage:
CH13           IF (totalCash <= 0) THEN
CH05              PRINT "Too bad. Hope you have a ticket home."
                  PRINT "Come back when you've got more money."
CH13           ELSE
CH05              PRINT "You are leaving with money, which is more than"
                  PRINT "I can say for a lot of people!  Good-bye!"
CH13           END IF
CH22           RETURN
            END

CH24        SUB doWinSound
CH04        ' Generates a rising sound for a winning combination
CH16           FOR tone = 1000 TO 10000 STEP 450
CH25              SOUND tone, 1
               NEXT tone
```

```
CH24    END SUB

CH24    SUB drawBar (colPos%, rowPos%)
CH04    ' Draws a yellow bar

CH26      LINE (colPos%, rowPos%)-(colPos% + 80, rowPos% + 30), 14, B
CH27      PAINT (colPos% + 1, rowPos% + 1), 14, 14
CH08      COLOR 15, 1 ' Reset screen to white letters, blue background
CH24    END SUB

CH24    SUB drawCherry (colPos%, rowPos%)
CH04    ' Draws a cherry with a stem
        ' Adjust for cherry's shape
CH10      colPos% = colPos% + 35
          rowPos% = rowPos% + 10
          ' cherry outline
CH26      CIRCLE (colPos%, rowPos%), 6, 4
          CIRCLE (colPos% - 7, rowPos% + 3), 6, 4
          CIRCLE (colPos% - 1, rowPos% + 6), 6, 4
          ' red color
CH27      PAINT (colPos% + 1, rowPos%), 4, 4
          PAINT (colPos% - 7, rowPos% + 3), 4, 4
          PAINT (colPos%, rowPos% + 6), 4, 4
          ' stem
CH26      LINE (colPos%,rowPos% + 2)-(colPos% + 20,rowPos% + 4), 4, B
CH27      PAINT (colPos% + 19, rowPos% + 3), 2, 4
CH24    END SUB

CH24    SUB drawPlum (colPos%, rowPos%)
CH04    ' Draws a purple plum
        ' Adjust for plum shape
CH10      colPos% = colPos% + 20
          rowPos% = rowPos% + 20

CH26      CIRCLE (colPos% + 19, rowPos% - 5), 18, 13
CH27      PAINT (colPos% + 19, rowPos% - 5), 13, 13
CH26      LINE (colPos% + 37, rowPos%)-(colPos% + 39, rowPos% + 2), 6
CH26      PSET (colPos% + 19, rowPos% - 9), 0
          PSET (colPos% + 24, rowPos% - 8), 0
          PSET (colPos% + 27, rowPos% - 6), 0
          PSET (colPos% + 25, rowPos% - 4), 0
CH24    END SUB

CH24    SUB finalSpin (totalCash)
CH04    ' Generates a final spin and adds to total if a winning
        ' combination
```

```
CH05        CLS
CH08        COLOR 15, 1
CH16        FOR i = 1 TO 3
CH11        n = INT(3 * RND) + 1
CH14        SELECT CASE n
                CASE 1
CH24                CALL drawBar(i * 130, 130)
                    numBars = numBars + 1
                CASE 2
CH24                CALL drawPlum(i * 130, 130)
                    numPlums = numPlums + 1
                CASE 3
CH24                CALL drawCherry(i * 130, 130)
                    numCherries = numCherries + 1
                END SELECT
            NEXT i
CH13        IF numBars = 3 THEN              ' 3 bars printed
CH24            CALL doWinSound
CH05            PRINT "Three bars!  You Win $2.00!!"
CH10            totalCash = totalCash + 2!
CH13        ELSEIF numPlums = 3 THEN         ' 3 plums printed
CH24            CALL doWinSound
CH05            PRINT "Three plums!  You Win $2.50!!"
CH06            totalCash = totalCash + 2.5
CH13        ELSEIF numCherries = 3 THEN      ' 3 cherries printed
CH24            CALL doWinSound
CH05            PRINT "Three cherries!  You Win $3.00!!"
CH10            totalCash = totalCash + 3!
CH13        END IF

CH24        END SUB

CH24        SUB spinReels
CH16        FOR spin = 1 TO 3
CH24            CALL drawPlum(130, 130)
                CALL drawCherry(260, 130)
                CALL drawBar(390, 130)
CH25            SOUND INT(RND * 8000) + 37, 1.82
CH05            CLS
CH08            COLOR 15, 1
CH24            CALL drawPlum(390, 130)
                CALL drawCherry(130, 130)
                CALL drawBar(260, 130)
CH25            SOUND INT(RND * 8000) + 37, 1.82
CH05            CLS
CH08            COLOR 15, 1
```

CH24
```
        CALL drawPlum(260, 130)
        CALL drawCherry(390, 130)
        CALL drawBar(130, 130)
```
CH25 `        SOUND INT(RND * 8000) + 37, 1.82`
CH05 `        CLS`
CH08 `        COLOR 15, 1`
```
    NEXT spin
```

CH24 `    END SUB`

ASCII Chart

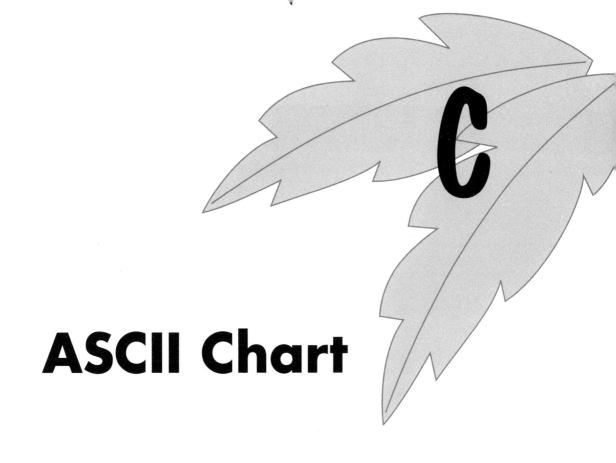

Dec	ASCII Character
000	null
001	☺
002	☻
003	♥
004	♦
005	♣
006	♠
007	●
008	■
009	○
010	■
011	♂
012	♀
013	♪
014	♪♪
015	☼
016	►

Dec	ASCII Character
017	◄
018	↕
019	‼
020	¶
021	§
022	▬
023	↨
024	↑
025	↓
026	→
027	←
028	FS
029	GS
030	RS
031	US
032	SP
033	!
034	"
035	#
036	$
037	%
038	&
039	'
040	(
041	)
042	*
043	+
044	,
045	-
046	.
047	/

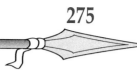

Dec	ASCII Character
048	0
049	1
050	2
051	3
052	4
053	5
054	6
055	7
056	8
057	9
058	:
059	;
060	<
061	=
062	>
063	?
064	@
065	A
066	B
067	C
068	D
069	E
070	F
071	G
072	H
073	I
074	J
075	K
076	L
077	M
078	N

Dec	ASCII Character
079	O
080	P
081	Q
082	R
083	S
084	T
085	U
086	V
087	W
088	X
089	Y
090	Z
091	[
092	\
093	]
094	^
095	_
096	`
097	a
098	b
099	c
100	d
101	e
102	f
103	g
104	h
105	i
106	j
107	k
108	l
109	m

Dec	ASCII Character
110	n
111	o
112	p
113	q
114	r
115	s
116	t
117	u
118	v
119	w
120	x
121	y
122	z
123	{
124	¦
125	}
126	~
127	DEL
128	Ç
129	ü
130	é
131	â
132	ä
133	à
134	å
135	ç
136	ê
137	ë
138	è
139	ï
140	î

Dec	ASCII Character
141	ì
142	Ä
143	Å
144	É
145	æ
146	Æ
147	ô
148	ö
149	ò
150	û
151	ù
152	ÿ
153	Ö
154	Ü
155	¢
156	£
157	¥
158	P$_t$
159	ƒ
160	á
161	í
162	ó
163	ú
164	ñ
165	Ñ
166	a
167	o
168	¿
169	⌐
170	¬
171	½

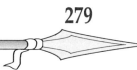

Dec	ASCII Character
172	¼
173	¡
174	«
175	»
176	▒
177	▓
178	█
179	│
180	┤
181	╡
182	╢
183	╖
184	╕
185	╣
186	║
187	╗
188	╝
189	╜
190	╛
191	┐
192	└
193	┴
194	┬
195	├
196	─
197	┼
198	╞
199	╟
200	╚
201	╔
202	╩

Dec	ASCII Character
203	╦
204	╠
205	═
206	╬
207	╧
208	╨
209	╤
210	╥
211	╙
212	╘
213	╒
214	╓
215	╫
216	╪
217	┘
218	┌
219	█
220	▄
221	▌
222	▐
223	▀
224	α
225	β
226	Γ
227	π
228	Σ
229	σ
230	μ
231	τ
232	Φ
233	θ

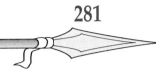

Dec	ASCII Character
234	Ω
235	δ
236	∞
237	ø
238	∈
239	∩
240	≡
241	±
242	≥
243	≤
244	⌠
245	⌡
246	÷
247	≈
248	°
249	•
250	·
251	√
252	η
253	2
254	■
255	

HMM...

The last 128 ASCII codes listed in this table (numbers 128 through 255) are specific to IBM PCs and IBM compatibles.

Index

Add to Your Sams Library Today with the Best Books for Programming, Operating Systems, and New Technologies

The easiest way to order is to pick up the phone and call

1-800-428-5331

between 9:00 a.m. and 5:00 p.m. EST.

For faster service please have your credit card available.

ISBN	Quantity	Description of Item	Unit Cost	Total Cost
0-672-30341-8		Absolute Beginner's Guide to C	$16.95	
0-672-30326-4		Absolute Beginner's Guide to Networking	$19.95	
0-672-30282-9		Absolute Beginner's Guide to Memory Management	$16.95	
0-672-30040-0		Teach Yourself C in 21 Days	$24.95	
0-672-30280-2		Turbo C++ Programming 101 (Book/Disk)	$29.95	
0-672-30080-X		Moving from C to C++	$29.95	
0-672-30319-1		The Waite Group's New C Primer Plus, 2E	$29.95	
0-672-48518-4		C Programming for UNIX	$29.95	
0-672-30259-4		Do-It-Yourself Visual Basic for Windows, 2E	$24.95	
0-672-30281-0		QBasic Programming 101 (Book/Disk)	$29.95	
0-672-30288-8		DOS Secrets Unleashed (Book/Disk)	$39.95	
0-672-30324-8		Teach Yourself QBasic in 21 Days	$24.95	
0-672-30200-4		C++ Programming 101 (Book/Disk)	$29.95	
0-672-30285-3		Turbo Pascal Programming 101 (Book/Disk)	$29.95	
0-672-30310-8		Windows Graphics FunPack (Book/Disk)	$19.95	
0-672-30318-3		Windows Sound FunPack (Book/Disk)	$19.95	
❏ 3 ½" Disk		Shipping and Handling: See information below.		
❏ 5 ¼" Disk		TOTAL		

Shipping and Handling: $4.00 for the first book, and $1.75 for each additional book. Floppy disk: Add $1.75 for shipping and handling. If you need to have it NOW, we can ship the product to you in 24 hours for an additional charge of approximately $18.00, and you will receive your item overnight or in two days. Overseas shipping and handling: Add $2.00 per book and $8.00 for up to three disks. Prices subject to change. Call for availability and pricing information on latest editions.

11711 N. College Avenue, Suite 140, Carmel, Indiana 46032

1-800-428-5331 — Orders   1-800-835-3202 — FAX   1-800-858-7674 — Customer Service

Book ISBN 0-672-30342-6